CONTENTS

Growing Vegetables   4

• The versatile vegetable   • Preparing a vegetable plot
• Planning your crops   • Natural ways of protecting plants
• Container gardens   • Cooking vegetables

Popular Vegetables   12

• A–Z of 50 popular vegetables from artichoke
to zucchini

Storing Vegetables   74

• How to store fresh vegetables
• A separate entry for each vegetable

Freezing Vegetables   78

• How to freeze vegetables
• A separate entry for each vegetable

Harvesting Chart   82

• When to harvest—spring, summer, winter or autumn
• Includes all climate zones

Harvest Recipes   84

• Delicious ways to cook, store and preserve
excess vegetables at harvest time

Index   94

LEFT: The vegetable garden need not be relaxed and casual. It can be more structured and formal as in this charming traditional garden.

GROWING VEGETABLES

Even the tiniest space in your garden, or a pot or container, will yield some of your favorite vegetables once you know how easy it is to grow them.

Growing, harvesting, preparing and eating food from your own garden is all part of the same activity and a wonderfully rewarding experience. It should be a grand celebration from garden to table, and the purpose of this book is to show you just how easy it is to grow your own vegetables, wherever you live. Your favorite vegetables will taste particularly flavorful and be more nutritious when freshly picked just prior to eating or cooking.

ABOVE: *This chocolate brown pepper has a similar flavor to the red and green varieties and looks spectacular in salads.*

LEFT: *Beds are raised and rambling vines confined to outer fence boundaries in this well-planned flower and vegetable garden.*

A GARDEN BED, HEAVILY MULCHED WITH STRAW *to discourage weed growth and keep soil surface temperature evenly cool. Mulching not only keeps the soil healthy but also makes less work for the home vegetable gardener.*

THE VERSATILE VEGETABLE

What is a vegetable? For all intents and purposes it is the edible part of any herbaceous plant and so includes all parts of the plant such as the roots, bulbs, tubers, stems, leaves, flowers, as well as seeds and fruits.

Without getting too technical about it, fruits used as vegetables include tomato, pepper, eggplant, cucumber, melon, squash and pumpkin. Stems or shoots include celery, asparagus, Swiss chard, leeks and rhubarb. Leafy vegetables, eaten either raw or cooked, include cabbage, spinach, lettuce, endive and Brussels sprouts.

We eat the roots, bulbs and tubers of carrots, parsnips, beets, rutabaga, turnips, onions and potatoes. Seeds are eaten as vegetables in the mature or immature state and include green peas, snow and sugar snap peas, sweet corn and broad beans. Flowers known as vegetables include the cauliflower, globe artichoke and broccoli.

PREPARING A VEGETABLE PLOT

Vegetable gardens may be of any shape or size, but regardless of design, they must be in a position to receive sunlight for the greater part of the day and have protection against wind. Keep clear of trees and other garden plants that will compete for water and nutrients. If topsoil is shallow or of poor quality, beds should be raised and well drained to allow root growth and prevent waterlogging after heavy rains.

Soil preparation

Heavy soils such as clay and clay loams should not be worked while wet, rather left to dry out to the crumbly stage. To improve these types of soil, add lime in the form of gypsum (calcium sulfate) which will improve the soil and allow other essential elements such as sulfur and phosphorus to be taken up ' the plant. Organic matter in the form of animal m   res, decaying straw, sawdust or compost is essential to b   .. down heavy soils and increase root penetration. It has

the added advantage of providing some of the nutrients required by vegetables.

Sandy soils require very little digging but have practically no water retention qualities. This can be improved with the addition of compost and regular additions of mulch or leaf mold to the soil surface. While some do not like the appearance, grass clippings make an excellent mulch and can be applied directly to the beds (but not too thickly) or ´ incorporated into the compost heap.

Maintaining pH levels

Most vegetables grow best in soils that have a pH range of between 6.0 and 7.0. The pH scale is one by which the acidity or alkalinity of soil is measured. It ranges between 1 and 14, pH 7 representing neutral, figures below representing increasing acidity and those above, to pH 14, increasing alkalinity. The range can vary from climate to climate and you would be well advised to check levels before planting.

Most vegetables do best in slightly acidic soils so if you are serious about growing healthy crops, invest in an inexpensive pH testing kit. These can be purchased from most garden centers. Gardens like regular applications of lime to maintain ideal pH levels. Lime contains an essential nutrient, calcium. It is easily lost from the soil, especially in areas of high rainfall and will constantly need replacing. An annual application of between 2 and 4 oz per square yard is usually sufficient to remedy this. If you are a keen organic gardener, it is not advisable to mix lime with animal manure. This causes a release of ammonia gas and consequent loss of nitrogen. Lime is returned to the soil by adding it or wood ash to the compost heap rather than digging directly into the soil.

These days, commercially available garden lime often contains quantities of trace elements as well. The uptake of trace elements and other nutrients will only occur within certain pH ranges. Nitrogen, phosphorus, calcium and magnesium for example, need a neutral to slightly alkaline pH range for their uptake, whereas iron, manganese and boron need a slightly acidic soil. Nevertheless, even though pH levels may remain constant, remember that it is humus and other decaying organic matter in the soil that bacteria feed on which in turn makes nutrients and trace elements available to the plant. Diseases indicating these nutritional shortages will soon manifest themselves if the soil is not rich in humus.

Mulching

Mulch is the covering you place over garden soil to keep it healthy, to discourage weed growth and keep the surface temperature evenly cool. With heavy soils, it makes them less compact and therefore increases aeration throughout the soil. With sandy soils, it contributes nutrients and increases moisture absorption. Black, opaque plastic sheeting is a non-organic mulch that can be used where crops need warm soils, but watering then becomes a problem. Irrigation systems under the sheet may have to be installed.

Organic mulching materials such as leaves, compost, straw, lawn clippings and sawdust have their problems as well as benefits. They should be in a state of decay when used to avoid compaction and nitrogen deprivation of surrounding plants. Extra nitrogen may have to be added to soil and new mulch added from time to time.

Fertilizers

Vegetables grown in the garden require fertilizers at one time or another. Composting is not the complete answer as it will only contain those elements present in the composted material. Organic gardeners will use only "natural" products such as bone meal and animal manures, but these are usually short of phosphorus, with the exception of fowl manure. Commercial fertilizers contain the three main elements, nitrogen (N), phosphorus (P) and potassium (K), required by plants for healthy growth. They are applied at different times of the year and in varying quantities, depending on the type of vegetable grown, the composition of the soil and previous use of other fertilizers. The proportions in which these elements are combined is known as the NPK ratio. Complete fertilizers are usually applied before or at time of planting and should be thoroughly incorporated into the top 4 in of soil. Use about 2 oz of fertilizer per 1 yard row.

Side dressings of additional fertilizer or the application of supplementary foliar fertilizers, which also contain trace

RAISED GARDEN BEDS *need careful watering to avoid water loss.*

A CAREFULLY PLANNED GARDEN *will make the most effective use of the available space.*

elements needed by the plant, may be required during the growing period.

Preparing garden beds

Raised-bed gardening is a compromise between gardening beds and containers. It can also solve the problem of localized poor soils and drainage. New soil should be about 20 in above surrounding soil levels and confined to beds approximately 1 yard wide framed by railway sleepers, rocks or other strong construction material. Moisture levels in raised-bed gardens should be carefully monitored as they tend to dry out faster than normal ground-level beds.

PLANNING YOUR CROPS

Greater yields will be obtained and a greater number of vegetables harvested if you put a little thought into planning your crops. The following factors need to be considered and will determine the sorts of vegetables you choose to grow.
● What is the climate like in your particular area: tropical, warm or cold?
● When is the best time for you to plant, and when should you harvest?
● Is it best for you to sow seed or plant seedlings?
● How much space is there in your garden, and do you have suitable soil?
● Do you need to build supporting trellises for your plants?

Climate

Choose crops according to the climate. How hot will it get and how cold will it get over the growing seasons? Vegetables generally do well in the 40–85°F range. In warm temperatures plant growth increases and in cold temperatures plant growth slows down. Leafy crops such as lettuce or cabbage, for example, will go to seed and flower too early in hot climates. On the other hand, if temperatures drop, especially at night,

VEGETABLES TO GROW IN COOL SEASON

Artichokes, globe and Jerusalem	Kohlrabi
Asparagus	Leek
Broad beans	Lettuce
Broccoli	Parsnip
Brussels sprouts	Peas
Cabbage	Potato
Carrots	Radish
Cauliflower	Rutabaga
Celery	Shallot
Chinese cabbage	Silver beet
Endive	Spinach
	Turnip
	Witloof

when frosts might develop, some vegetables such as peppers may drop their flowers and no fruit will develop. In both cases, the end result is reduced yields.

Planting and harvesting

In general, planting dates depend on how hardy the plant is and how it will tolerate the cold weather. It is wise, therefore, to plan which are the cool and warm season crops suitable for your particular area. Cool season crops need time to mature before warm weather, otherwise they will go to seed. Warm season crops do not like frosts and usually are deeper rooting and have larger leaves than cool season vegetables. They can, therefore, tolerate drier conditions.

Harvesting dates, that is the number of days from planting to maturity, vary from vegetable to vegetable. Some can be picked early, some mid-season and others late in the season (see chart page 82–3).

Seeds and seedlings

The choice is yours and much depends on available space and time factors. Seeds may be sown direct into the garden bed or raised to the seedling stage in seed beds, containers or seed boxes. Seedlings may be planted directly into the garden or in containers.

If planting seeds directly into the soil, open up a narrow planting row 4 in deep and 4 in wide. Spread complete fertilizer along the trench, then fill in with soil. Sow seeds on top of the soil, then cover with a thin film of enriched soil containing coarse sand to prevent compaction and allow easy passage for the shoots on germination. Tamp down and keep soil moist but not wet. It may be necessary to water gently twice a day. Provide some protection from both extreme heat and heavy rain for the emerging seedlings in open seed beds. Polythene mesh on wooden frames is ideal for this purpose.

Alternatively, seedlings can be raised in one of the many varieties of containers that are available. The advantage is that you provide a protective and controlled environment for the developing plant which will be quite sturdy when you come to transplant it into the open garden. If raising seedlings in

containers, use a potting mix made up of equal parts of sand or sandy loam and peat moss. Vermiculite is a good substitute for the latter. For every quart of this soil mixture, add $1/3$ oz of complete fertilizer NPK 5:7:4, $1/10$ oz bone meal, and $1/8$ oz dolomite (lime). After planting in containers fertilize weekly with a soluble form of complete fertilizer.

Planting—space, soil and support

Access to sunlight is vital, and it is wise to watch where the sun penetrates surrounding buildings, shrubbery and fences throughout the day before choosing your garden site. On sloping ground, beds may need support with rocks or other construction material. Check the condition of the soil: does it need the addition of fertilizers, animal manures or compost?

The type of vegetables you plant will depend entirely on your own needs and preferences. High-yielding or quick-maturing, exotic or hard-to-get varieties are just some of the choices you will have to make. Use surrounding fences to support peas or climbing beans. Keep taller plants, such as staked tomatoes or peppers, and leafy vegetables, such as rhubarb, broad beans or spinach, to the back rows. Smaller vegetables, such as carrots, beets and lettuce, can be grown towards the front, and the garden bordered by herbs such as parsley.

Consult seasonal growing charts to replace one quick-growing vegetable with another throughout the year. This will ensure a constant supply of fresh produce from your vegetable garden.

Succession planting

Plan carefully where garden space is limited and you want to harvest a variety of crops over the growing season from the same small area. Begin your succession planting with a fast-growing, cool season crop such as spinach or lettuce followed by warm weather vegetables such as sweet corn, squash or okra. Then in autumn plant root crops such as beets, rutabaga or turnips. Use your trellis space wisely, perhaps by planting peas in the cool season and cucumbers in the hot months.

In larger gardens where space is not at a premium, succession planting, or crop rotation, is an advisable practice. Do not plant two successive crops of the same or related vegetables in the same area. For example, alternate root crops such as carrots or beets with leguminous vegetables such as peas or beans. Rotation of crops in this way will reduce the build-up of pests and diseases in the soil and lead to the growth of healthy vegetables.

VEGETABLES TO GROW IN WARM SEASON

Beans, green	Peppers
Chayote	Pumpkin
Cucumber	Spinach
Eggplant	Squash
Fennel	Sweet corn
Lettuce	Sweet potato
Okra	Tomato

WELL-PLANNED ROWS OF VEGETABLES *make valuable use of limited garden areas and look very attractive. Alternatively, you may wish to have a more natural-looking vegetable garden where vegetables are planted in a less formal pattern (see Permaculture, page 10).*

NATURAL WAYS OF PROTECTING PLANTS

All plants need protection from pests and diseases. While chemicals are widely used, there are many natural or organic ways by which this can be achieved.

Companion planting

Plant compatibility is the basis of companion planting. It is an inexact science—many botanists will give it no credence at all! However, observation by gardeners over the years has shown that some vegetables and herbs will grow better when near others and some will look decidedly sick or not grow at all. In their natural environment many plants, left alone to self-seed from season to season, establish particular relationships, one with the other, small shallow-rooting ones growing in the shade of larger neighbors that protect them from the harsh, drying sun.

The opposite to this can be seen in monocultures, such as market gardens or orchards, where the same types of plants are grown together to produce a specific crop. If a disease, fungus or pest, particular to that variety, takes hold then trouble ensues for the entire area.

Many gardeners believe companion planting plays a role in the control of pests and diseases in the vegetable garden. Some also maintain that it is better not to use artificial or chemically manufactured insecticides, herbicides and fungicides, and practice companion planting as an alternative.

Sometimes, to save a crop, the use of sprays may be unavoidable. Wherever possible, use "natural" sprays (see below) to keep your vegetables disease- and pest-free.

Vegetables or herbs may exude natural chemicals that either attract or repel insects or other plants. Members of the *Allium* group, such as chives and garlic, are believed to stunt the growth of peas or beans when grown nearby. They will also repel aphids when planted near roses or deter the growth of apple scab when planted under apple trees, although considerations of scale come into it. How can a small chive save a big apple tree? Best to incorporate the onions or chives into a natural spray and apply this to the apple tree foliage.

Natural sprays

Herbs have great aromatic qualities which, when released in the form of a spray, can control many pests. It is important to note that natural sprays may have harmful side effects, and that care needs to be taken with their storage and usage. Always store in clearly labeled childproof containers out of the reach of children. Rhubarb spray is particularly toxic and after its use harvesting should be withheld for two weeks. With other natural sprays withhold harvest for 24 hours.

General all-purpose spray

Gather as many herbs as you can muster. If possible, include rosemary, thyme, marjoram, sage, parsley, borage, mints, basil, chives, chamomile, and pyrethrum and tansy. Place in a large pot, cover with water and bring to the boil. Remove pot from the stove, cover and let the herbs infuse in the water as it cools. Strain and use as a spray in the vegetable garden.

Garlic spray

Mix together in 2 cups water 2 cloves chopped garlic, 1 tablespoon pure soap powder and 2 tablespoons paraffin oil.

ZUCCHINI WILL *grow well in a medium-sized container, showing off its striking flowers and soft, attractive leaves.*

annual and perennial plants, animals, soils, water management, and human needs into intricately connected, productive communities." (*Introduction to Permaculture*, 1991).

The layout of the vegetable and herb garden in permaculture terms is not a fixed or rigid thing. Rather, is it based on how many times you may visit the garden and the size and variety of crops grown. Garden beds may be placed in close proximity to the house for easy access. This form of garden provides conditions of both light and shade as well as good drainage and plants are grown to fit in with the environment. Tomatoes, eggplant or beans can be placed in narrow beds against supporting structures. Nearby you may consider placing quick-growing salad vegetables, such as chives, cress or rocket.

CONTAINER GARDENS

Even in the smallest of confined spaces you can grow small crops of vegetables given the right conditions. Containers, which come in many shapes and sizes, are ideal.

The method is particularly important for those with physical disabilities, who are unable to work large gardens yet appreciate a supply of fresh produce near the home. It is equally important in areas where soil pollution may prevent the healthy cultivation of crops.

Planter boxes, wooden barrels, hanging baskets, and terracotta, concrete or plastic pots are just some of the containers that can be used. Here are some basic rules to follow.

● Do not use galvanised containers or any pot with a narrow opening.
● Cheap plastic pots may deteriorate in UV sunlight and terracotta pots dry out rapidly. Glazed ceramic pots are excellent but require more than one drainage hole.
● Wooden barrels or containers should be treated with preservative before planting to prevent timber rot.
● Use containers of between 15 and 120 quarts capacity. Small pots restrict the root area and dry out very quickly.

Set aside in a cool space for 2–3 days, then strain and bottle. When ready to use as a spray, dilute 1 part of garlic solution in 50 parts of water. Garlic spray can be used on plants affected by aphids, caterpillars or fungal diseases.

Rhubarb spray
This is quite lethal to sucking insects. Rhubarb leaves are poisonous and care must be taken with this spray. Keep out of the reach of children, and withhold harvesting vegetables for two weeks after spraying. To make, chop and boil 10 large rhubarb leaves in 3 quarts of water for 30 minutes. Add ½ oz pure soap powder and stir until dissolved. Cool, then strain.

Chamomile tea
Gather together 1 cup of chamomile flowers and soak in a bowl of cold water for 3 days. Strain, then spray on young plants that begin to droop. It is most effective on young container-grown seedlings, reducing the "damping-off" effect.

Soap spray
This is an easy mixture to put together when nothing else is available. The spray works by coating insects with a thin film and suffocates them—a procedure that may need to be repeated several times. After the insects have dropped off the plant, rinse the leaves with fresh water. Mealy bug, scale, aphids and caterpillars can be treated in this way. The spray is made by mixing ⅔ oz pure soap powder in 2 quarts of water.

Permaculture
Permaculture is a contraction of the words "permanent agriculture," a system created and named by the biologist and naturalist Bill Mollison. It is " ... a philosophy and an approach to land use which weaves together microclimate,

CHERRY TOMATOES AND BASIL *grow companionably in plastic and ceramic container pots.*

A BRILLIANT RANGE *of colors and textures of vegetables at their finest. Careful cooking will enhance these characteristics.*

Deep-rooting vegetables require deep containers.

● Provide adequate drainage holes, about 1/2 in across, and line the base of the pot with newspaper or layers of garden shade cloth to prevent loss of soil. There is no need to place gravel or pottery pieces in the container.

● Use light-colored containers in preference to black in hot climates to lessen heat absorption and uneven root growth.

● The size or number of vegetables to be grown will determine size of container used.

● Containers should be set on bricks or blocks to allow for free drainage.

● Hanging baskets can be lined with layers of sphagnum moss for water retention. Keep baskets away from afternoon sun and shelter them from heavy winds.

Soils and potting mixes

Buy a good quality commercial potting mix which will be free of unwanted seeds and soil-borne diseases. Most garden soils are usually too heavy and are unsuitable for container growing. Soils should be lightweight and moisture-retentive (peat moss is ideal), yet moderately fast in drainage time. The desired pH range is 5.6 to 7.0.

Cultivation

It is quicker to grow from plants than from seeds. Firm the soil around the roots of the plants and set them about 2 in in from the edge of the container, leaving 2 in of space between the surface of the soil and the rim of the container.

Always use a light spray fitting on your hose to increase water and soil retention around plants. Because potting mixes

are acidic, lime and fertilizers will need to be added to soil throughout the growing period. Weekly applications of liquid fertilizer are recommended. After planting, cover topsoil with a 1/2 in layer of mulch, but keep it just clear of leafy vegetables such as lettuce, which are susceptible to rot.

What to grow in containers

Small salad greens such as oak leaf lettuce and mustard cress, or vegetables such as silver beet, which have a quick maturing period, are ideal. Cherry tomatoes and other fruiting vegetables, including peppers or eggplant, can be easily grown in containers, as can root vegetables such as baby carrots, radishes or spring onions.

Much the same conditions for watering and fertilizing apply to container-grown herbs as to vegetables grown in containers. Combine faster-growing herbs around slower-growing vegetables such as broccoli, although you will need to match the seasonal growth of the different plants.

COOKING VEGETABLES

Vegetables offer a nutritious and tasty way to balance the diet and provide many of the vitamins and minerals essential to health. Nature ensures variety because a different vegetable will reach its peak harvesting time every month of the year. Let the seasons be your guide to cheap, flavorful food.

Cooking times vary according to the method used and the quality, size, quantity and freshness of the vegetables. Whenever possible cook vegetables in their skins.

● The healthiest way to cook vegetables is in the microwave using very little water. This will retain most nutrients. Washed leafy vegetables need no extra water when microwaved as the water on the leaves is sufficient.

● To steam, cook vegetables in an enclosed container suspended over a small amount of boiling water.

● Boiling involves completely immersing vegetables in boiling water or at least just covering them, and keeping the temperature constant until they are cooked. Water-soluble nutrients within the vegetable are leached out during this process, so do not waste the cooking water—use it later to make soups, stews and sauces.

● To parboil, boil vegetables for 5–8 minutes and then drain.

● Blanching involves covering the vegetable with boiling, salted water and cooking for a limited time. Fresh water is used for the second stage of cooking. Vegetables are sometimes blanched before freezing (see individual entries in Freezing Vegetables, pages 78–81).

● Glazing involves cooking in a small quantity of water, sugar and butter until the mixture is reduced to a syrup; stir frequently to avoid scorching. Beets, radishes, onions, parsnips and carrots lend themselves to glazing.

● Pureeing vegetables is done in the food processor or blender, or by pressing through a sieve by hand. Pureed vegetables can be eaten at once, or stored in the freezer and reconstituted later.

● Other techniques include sautéeing and deep-frying. Both of these methods bring the vegetable into direct contact with hot oils and so are very quick methods of cooking. Roasting is a much slower process but gives a delicious flavor.

ARTICHOKE

Cynara scolymus

PLENTY OF WATER *will ensure handsomely developed flower buds on the mature globe artichoke. Harvest before they begin to open.*

THISTLE-LIKE GLOBE ARTICHOKE *bushes need plenty of room but make attractive companions for other plants in the garden.*

FEATURES

Globe artichoke is a gray-green perennial 3–4 ft tall with decorative compound leaves resembling those of the Scottish thistle. Edible parts are the young, tender, globe-shaped flower buds which are harvested and eaten before opening.

CONDITIONS

Climate Best grown in areas with mild relatively frost-free winters and damp cool summers. Ideal range is 50°F at night to 74°F by day.

Aspect Prefers full sun in rich well-drained soils.

Cultivation Soil should be enriched and prepared with fertilizer and animal compost to improve drainage. Keep mulch and water up to plants in growing season and in summer after harvesting. In autumn in cool areas needs to be cut back to 10–12 in and heavily mulched to protect root structure in winter.

GROWING METHOD

Planting Obtain shoots or suckers of disease-resistant varieties from nurseries. Success from planting from seed is variable and takes about one year between sowing and harvesting. Plant in spring in subtropical areas, in late winter in warm regions, and in midwinter in cooler climates. As artichokes require plenty of space to allow for spreading growth, place in beds 3 ft apart and in rows approximately 3 ft apart.

Watering Keep soils evenly and constantly moist, carefully monitoring this throughout the spring and summer months.

Fertilizing Prepare garden beds with low nitrogen fertilizer NPK 5:10:10 spread at a rate of 1 lb per 9 square yards. Repeat this application again at mid-season. At planting time, apply half a cup of fertilizer around each shoot or sucker.

Problems Good drainage during growth is essential otherwise crown rot may develop, principally as a result of the heavy mulching requirement over winter. Handle the plants as little as possible and remove any infected or diseased specimens immediately.

HARVESTING

Picking Artichokes take 2–3 months to reach maturity from time of planting when grown from shoots or suckers, and approximately a year if grown from seed. In many areas, harvesting takes place from mid to late spring when buds are tight and about 3 in across. Cut well below the bud with 1 in of stem still attached. The optimum bearing period is the second year after planting, with adult plants being divided and replanted every third year.

ASPARAGUS
Asparagus officinalis

FERN-LIKE FEATHERY FOLIAGE, *which is one of the characteristic features of the asparagus plant, can be seen here. Growing among the foliage are mature green spears as well as purplish immature spears just protruding above soil level.*

FEATURES

Attractive fern-like feathery foliage is a feature of this hardy perennial which grows to 3 ft tall. The edible part of the plant is the tender young stem or spear. Male and female flowers grow on separate plants, with male plants producing larger and better spears. Female plants, identified by their red berries, should be discarded after second autumn of growth. This delicious vegetable is easy to grow.

CONDITIONS

Climate Grows well in mild to cold climates and can withstand frosts, which fit in with dormancy period.

Aspect Prefers full sun but will grow in partial shade. Well-drained soil pH 6+ is required in prepared garden beds. Not suitable for container growing.

Cultivation Prepare permanent beds to depth 14 in with plenty of organic matter and a complete fertilizer 1 lb per 9 square yards. Dig trench 10 in wide and 10 in deep. Set crowns 16 in apart in trench; cover with 2 in soil. As fern grows, cover with soil until trench is filled, leaving new shoots uncovered. For "white" or blanched asparagus, mound soil over trenches to depth of 10–12 in in late winter. Fern dies off in winter and new shoots occur in spring.

GROWING METHOD

Planting Plant seeds in spring in special beds. Transfer two-year-old seedlings during winter or spring to permanent position. Alternatively, buy and plant two-year-old crowns in winter.

Watering Keep soil moist, especially when spears are forming. Dry soil causes stringy, woody stalks.

Fertilizing Apply regular applications of high nitrogen fertilizer NPK 10:4:6 at a rate of 1 lb per 9 square yards in summer to encourage top growth, and late winter for spring spear growth.

Problems Mostly problem free. Grow rust-resistant varieties to lessen incidence of rust. Spray for asparagus beetle if this becomes a problem.

HARVESTING

Picking Harvest three-year-old plant in late winter or early spring. Harvest period may last up to 8 weeks. Cut when spears are 6–8 in long at or just below soil level, being careful not to damage adjacent new shoots. Feathering of spear means harvest is too late. Harvest along same row at two week intervals in season. For white asparagus, cut spear 6 in below soil level when tip has just broken through surface. Production increases annually and maturity occurs at 4–5 years.

BEAN

Phaseolus vulgaris

THE REDDISH-PURPLE *flower of the French climbing bean is also edible. Bean flowers come in a range of lovely colors.*

THESE DWARF BEANS *have been mulched with a rich compost to protect the shallow root system and help them retain water.*

FEATURES

Annuals of both climbing and dwarf varieties have leaves composed of three small leaflets which are nutritious when used in salads. Edible flowers come in a variety of colors. The immature pod is the other edible part of this versatile vegetable. It can be green, yellow or purple, depending on variety, and comes in stringed and stringless forms. Climbing beans give a heavier crop over a longer period than dwarf varieties.

CONDITIONS

Climate A warm season vegetable which does not like frosts. In warmer subtropical climates it can be grown throughout the whole year.

Aspect Prefers sunny spots where the soil is warm. Climbing beans need a trellis or some other structure at least 8 ft tall for support.

Cultivation Cultivation for both dwarf and climbing beans is the same. Soils should be well drained and fertilized. Dig in plenty of organic matter if soil is too sandy. Mulch with compost to protect shallow root system and promote water retention. Hill rows with soil during early growth to protect against wind. When weeding take care not to disturb the soil or roots just beneath surface. Check with your nursery for suitable varieties for medium to large container growing.

GROWING METHOD

Planting Mid-spring through to late summer are the best times to plant, but whatever the region plant only after cold snaps are over and the danger of frost has passed. The growing season is short, around 10–12 weeks, and with high temperatures (over 60°F) pods may not set. Dwarf beans mature more quickly than climbing varieties, so stagger your planting to accommodate this. Sow seeds direct into beds with climbing beans 6 in apart in rows 3 ft apart; and dwarf varieties in rows 24 in apart with seeds at 2 in spacings.

Watering In sandy soils, watering is a must as beans have shallow root systems. Seeds sown in moist soils do not require further watering until the seedlings appear. At flowering time, beans like humid conditions. Water with a sprinkler in cooler climates.

Fertilizing If soil has low pH add 8 oz lime per square yard a month before sowing. Apply complete fertilizer NPK 5:6:6 as a 2 in wide layer either side of young plants. Or apply as a band, covered by soil, under newly sown seeds at rate of 2 oz per yard length of bed. Protect seeds from direct contact with fertilizer. Apply liquid fertilizer when flowering commences.

CLIMBING BEANS *growing on a pyramid structure of garden stakes. Some form of support is necessary for all climbing varieties.*

Problems   Aphids and red spider mite (midsummer to mid-autumn) and bean fly are the main pests, with blight mosaic and anthracnose being diseases to watch for. Control pests and diseases by spraying or dusting with insecticides, especially on undersides of leaves. Don't leave dead plant material lying around so as to avoid spreading disease. Seasonally rotate crops whenever possible so as to prevent the spread of disease.

HARVESTING

Picking   Dwarf beans will mature in about 10 weeks and climbing beans will be ready in 10–12 weeks. Frequent picking of beans will result in increased flowering as well as greater yields. However, be careful not to be too energetic when pulling the pods off so as not to damage the vines. The pods are ready to pick when they snap easily between the fingers and the seeds are not yet fully developed. Avoid harvesting in either very hot or cold spells.

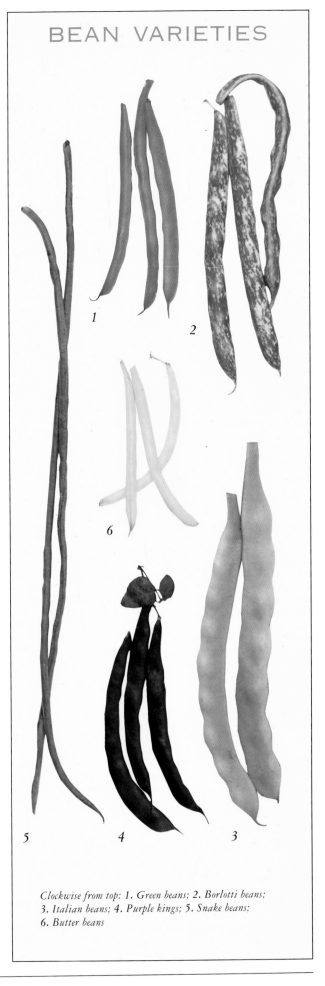

BEAN VARIETIES

Clockwise from top: 1. Green beans; 2. Borlotti beans; 3. Italian beans; 4. Purple kings; 5. Snake beans; 6. Butter beans

BEAN, BROAD
Vicia faba

THE YOUNG PODS *and pretty flowers of the broad bean are borne on stems which are an unusual square-shape.*

FEATURES

This is a hardy winter annual growing to 5 ft tall. It has square stems producing small leaflets which give the plant a bushy look. White flowers produce 6–8 in pods containing edible seeds in spring and early summer. The seeds are large and may be used fresh, although they are often also available in a dried form. This is a good vegetable to grow in the home garden as it is particularly easy to grow.

CONDITIONS

Climate   Grows very well in mild temperate and cool climates with temperatures below 68°F where cool weather helps to set the pods. Pods will not develop in areas which have very hot summers.

Aspect   Likes full sunlight in beds of alkaline soil that are well-drained and rich in organic matter.

Cultivation   Requires only limited attention during the 4–5 months growing season which plants take to reach maturity. They are ideal for small gardens but not really suited to container growing. If a good crop is evident, tips of growing shoots can be nipped out to hasten maturity.

GROWING METHOD

Planting   Sow seeds direct into bed where they will grow. Plant in early autumn in warm temperate climates, and autumn to winter in milder temperate to cooler zones. Rows should be at least 3 ft apart and seeds planted 2 in deep and 2 in apart within rows. Seeds take 18–20 weeks to reach maturity.

Fertilizing   As with other legumes, broad beans add atmospheric nitrogen to the soil through the action of nitrogen-fixing bacteria on their roots. By this action, they in a way produce their own fertilizer. When preparing beds dig in a base fertilizer NPK 5:8:4 at the rate of 5 oz per square yard. Too much fertilizer, especially in the form of animal manures, leads to pod-setting failure.

Watering   Do not overwater broad beans. In combination with high temperatures, wet soil conditions lead to root diseases. Seeds planted in damp soil require no watering until seedlings appear approximately two weeks later. As plant matures, water only when soil starts to dry out.

Problems   Aphids, tiny soft-bodied sucking insects, and small mites are the main pests and should be controlled by recommended insecticides or organically prepared garlic sprays. Diseases include rust and broad bean wilt, which causes darkening of the growing tip leading to wilting then death of the whole plant. Diseased plants should be removed and burned as quickly as possible. Protect remaining plants from aphids. Crop rotation over several seasons will lessen incidence of disease.

HARVESTING

Picking   Young pods can be harvested during early spring in most areas and the whole pod containing half-ripe seeds can be prepared and eaten as you would climbing beans. Otherwise, if left to mature and harvested when seeds are quite large, the seeds are removed from the pod and then used.

BEET

Beta vulgaris

THE TENDER *young red-veined leaves of the beet form a rosette shape. They make an attractive and nutritious addition to salads.*

THIS SWOLLEN ROOT *is ready for harvest. Beet grows at ground level and needs to be harvested before the plant goes to seed.*

FEATURES

Beets are mostly cultivated as an annual vegetable. The swollen edible root can be either rounded or tapered and is red, yellow (golden beet) or white. The leaves sprout as a rosette above ground and are delicious used in salads when young. Beets are suitable for growing in either gardens or large containers; however, the Cylindrica variety, with its long tubular roots, is not suitable for containers.

CONDITIONS

Climate Can grow in most climates although roots tend to become woody in regions with very hot weather. On the other hand, young plants may not develop roots and will go to seed if the weather becomes too cold. Watch planting times if you have these two extremes of temperature during the crucial stages of the growing season.

Aspect Can tolerate both sun and partial shade.

Cultivation Prefers loose soils, which allow root to grow freely. Soils need to be high in organic matter, well limed and with good drainage. Beets do not like weed competition but when weeding, take care not to damage developing roots.

GROWING METHOD

Planting Sow all season long in subtropical climates; during spring and autumn in warm regions, and spring through to early autumn in colder areas. Beets tolerate frost and grow best of all in cooler climates. Sow seeds direct into garden soil and stagger planting by a month for continuous supply throughout harvesting period. Prepare trenches 4 in deep, 3 in wide and in rows 16 in apart. Lay narrow band of complete fertilizer in trench and cover with 3 in of soil. Lay seeds on top then fill trench with more soil. Alternatively, dig in a complete fertilizer throughout bed before sowing. Thin very young seedlings to 1 in apart and later to 3 in as root swells.

Watering Give young beets plenty of water to encourage larger, tender roots. Left to dry out, the vegetable becomes tough and stringy.

Fertilizing In new beds, use a complete fertilizer NPK 6:6:6 at a rate of 2 oz per square yard. Do not over-manure or fertilize soils in beds that have been heavily fertilized for the previous crop as this leads to rather tasteless beets with a low sugar content.

Problems Seldom any problems.

HARVESTING

Picking Beets mature approximately 3–4 months after sowing, depending on area and seasonal conditions. Harvest before plant goes to seed and when root is sufficiently large.

BROCCOLI

Brassica oleracea var. *italica*

HARVEST THE LARGE *edible bud of broccoli before the flowers appear. Secondary buds will form once the central bud has been picked.*

FEATURES

Grown as an annual, broccoli looks like green cauliflower and it is also a member of the cabbage family. Flower stalks are green, purplish to white in color and the plant has tiny yellow flowers. The edible part of broccoli is the head which is eaten when it is in bud and green with no yellow flowers showing.

CONDITIONS

Climate   Can be grown anywhere except in the hottest and coldest climates but does require a cool winter to reach maturity. Temperate and cold climates are therefore best with day temperatures not exceeding 77°F and night temperatures not below 60°F.

Aspect   Broccoli can be grown in containers on verandahs, or even indoors, as well as in beds that are well drained and have a sunny position in the garden.

Cultivation   Likes soil with a pH range of 6.5–7.5. Prepare garden beds with manures and fertilizers, providing extra nitrogen supplement if soil is sandy. Initial rapid leaf growth will occur, followed by development of the edible head in approximately 3–4 months. Side shoots develop after the central head has been harvested. New growth is encouraged if base of plant and some outer leaves are left on the plant after harvest.

GROWING METHOD

Planting   Sow seeds 3 in apart, ½ in deep, during late spring to early summer in cold climates, in late summer to autumn in warmer zones, and in autumn to winter in tropical areas. Successive sowings a month apart will produce a longer harvest period. To raise seedlings, grow in small 4 in pots. Transfer to garden beds planting 20 in apart when seedlings are 4 in tall and at least four true leaves have appeared. This takes about 6 weeks from when seeds are planted.

Watering   Plant grows quickly so keep soil moist by constant watering, if necessary. Cut down on watering as heads mature. Lack of moisture leads to seeding without head formation.

Fertilizing   Dig in 2 lbs poultry manure and 4 oz complete fertilizer NPK 6:6:6 per square yard. Additional fertilizing during growing season by application of side dressings of sulfate of ammonia leads to healthy plants. Weekly applications of liquid seaweed fertilizer also improve crops.

Problems   Broccoli is prone to disease. The risk will be reduced by seasonal crop rotation. The main insect pests are larvae of cabbage moth and white butterfly. These can be controlled with sprays or dustings containing *Bacillus thuringiensis* (a bioinsecticide) or pyrethrin. Curling of the leaf, a disease known as whip tail, is an indication of a trace element (molybdenum) shortage. Correct this deficiency by watering seedlings either before or after transplanting with a solution of ⅕ oz sodium molybdate in 5 quarts water. Downy mildew is also a condition to watch for in moist cool areas. If this is a problem see that the plant is well aerated and that there is maximum sunlight penetration.

HARVESTING

Picking   When buds are large and firm but not yet flowering, cut the large central head leaving about 6 in of stalk attached.

BRUSSELS SPROUT

Brassica oleracea var. *gemmifera*

THE TINY, CABBAGE-LIKE *brussels sprout loves the cooler weather but is very vulnerable to pests and diseases if neglected.*

FEATURES

The brussels sprout is a member of the cabbage family with similar requirements to those of cabbages. The small heads measure approximately 2 in in diameter, resemble cabbages and sprout from a tall main stem among large green leaves.

CONDITIONS

Climate Cool growing season is preferable. This hardy Brassica tolerates frosts but does not like either extended cold or hot periods. Not suitable for growing in hot subtropical climates. Areas with temperature range between 77°F by day and 50°F at night are ideal.

Aspect Garden beds should have a sunny aspect and be adequately drained. Brussels sprouts will not grow in waterlogged soils. Most soils suit with the exception of sandy soils which produce only loose leafy vegetables with no heart.

Cultivation The growing season is long, being approximately 5–6 months. Protect plants from wind damage by hilling soil around plants during the growing period. Removal of the terminal bud encourages sprouts to mature all at the same time. If you prefer the sprouts to ripen at the same time (see Picking notes), remove the terminal bud when the plant has reached the 16 in growth stage.

GROWING METHOD

Planting Sow seeds, well spaced, in seed trays. Transplant seedlings when 4 in tall during summer to autumn in cooler climates and during summer and early autumn in warm zones. Young plants will do best in soils of pH range 6.5–7.5.

Watering Water frequently as plants need a great deal of water as well as cool moist air to encourage growth. Ease off on watering a week or two before harvesting.

Fertilizing Prepare beds some weeks ahead of transplanting by digging in 2 lbs poultry manure with 2 oz complete fertilizer NPK 5:6:6 per square yard. Extra nitrogen can be added during picking times by the addition of sulfate of ammonia, $\frac{1}{3}$ oz per plant. If heavy rains have leached the soil, apply $\frac{1}{6}$ oz nitrate of potash per plant.

Problems This vegetable is very prone to pests and diseases. Cabbage moth causes problems early in the season and later aphids, slugs and snails may damage sprouts. Control these pests with commercial and/or organic sprays. Downy mildew and club root (intensified by acidic moist soil conditions) are diseases needing constant applications of fungicide. Yellowish areas around leaves are indicative of magnesium deficiency. Water soil around plant with a solution of 1 oz magnesium sulphate (Epsom salts) in 5 quarts water. Remember, many of these conditions can be avoided if proper drainage is provided in the first place. Proper preparation will prevent later problems.

HARVESTING

Picking Harvest period is late summer through to spring providing the weather is not too hot in which case harvest time will be shorter. Mature sprouts are harvested frequently, especially in warmer zones, and are picked before they burst, starting at the bottom of the stem where mature sprouts first develop.

CABBAGE
Brassica oleracea var. *capitata*

CABBAGES ARE *quite robust and not fussy about climate; they also store well. Leave the outer leaves attached to the stem when harvesting.*

FEATURES

This very hardy vegetable is grown as an annual right throughout the year. The edible head is a large terminal bud composed of many tightly packed, overlapping leaves forming a round or sometimes pointed head. The leaves are either green or purple, depending on variety, and have a smooth or crinkled texture. The stem is very short except when the plant is left to go to seed.

CONDITIONS

Climate Adaptable to a wide range of climates but basically a cool weather crop. It is frost-tolerant but not tolerant to extremes of heat which cause the head to split.

Aspect Prefers sunny well-drained beds that have been made fertile with the addition of decomposed animal or poultry manure and compost.

Cultivation Cabbages should be grown rapidly and kept well watered. A lot of watering also leads to a lot of leaching, depending on soil types, so keep garden beds well mulched. Biweekly applications of a nitrogen fertilizer may be necessary.

GROWING METHOD

Planting Plant in summer and spring in cool zones and all year round in other areas. First sow seeds ¼ in deep and 3 in apart in seed beds, then transplant into garden beds when seedlings are 5–6 weeks old, with 4 to 5 true leaves in evidence. Plant seedlings deeply, up to first leaves, 24 in apart in rows 32 in apart, depending on variety. Sugar loaf cabbages, for example, need only 12–16 in between plants. Harden off seedlings by withholding water for a couple of days just before transplanting.

Watering Cabbages like a lot of watering, so keep topsoil moist at all times.

Fertilizing Cabbages prefer slightly acid soils. Apply 7 oz dolomite along with 3½ oz complete fertilizer NPK 5:6:4 per square yard, several weeks before planting. Spread small amounts of the same fertilizer over the garden bed, one month after planting and water in at once. When cabbages start to form firm hearts, apply a light dressing of urea, ⅓ oz per square yard, especially if soils are sandy.

Problems Various kinds of caterpillars attack cabbages by eating holes in the leaves and eventually destroying the growing buds. These include caterpillars of the cabbage moth and white butterfly, the center grub and the corn ear worm. Spraying early in the season every 2 weeks from seedling stage onwards with an appropriate insecticide is recommended. Downy mildew and magnesium deficiency are common diseases. Treat them as for brussels sprout.

HARVESTING

Picking Cabbages take around 14–16 weeks to mature. In cool areas harvest in summer to autumn. In warm climates harvest in late spring through to early summer. Autumn and winter are the best harvest times for subtropical zones. Harvest when the head is firm, removing from the stem by cutting and leaving the outer leaves attached to the stem.

CARROT

Daucus carota

THE CARROT HAS *long been a favorite vegetable: it was first cultivated around the Mediterranean more than 2000 years ago.*

FEATURES

This hardy plant is grown as an annual. Round and short varieties may be grown in a container but the long tapering variety growing to 8 in requires friable soil in the open garden. "Baby" carrots grow no more than 4 in long and 3/4 in across. The underground root of the carrot is a strong golden orange producing a feathery green rosette of leaves above soil level.

CONDITIONS

Climate   Cold tolerant and preferring cooler zones, carrots can be grown in most climates.

Aspect   Likes full sun but tolerates partial shade. Prefers a garden bed positioned for coolness.

Cultivation   Older garden beds which have friable soils with decayed organic matter offer best results. Roots grow deep and smooth without blemishes in these sandy to loamy soils. Add lime if soils are acidic to improve root color. Keep weed free but avoid deep cultivation to protect developing roots and monitor moisture levels of soil. In sub-tropical zones may need to be mulched to keep soil cool. Companion planting with radishes will protect seedlings from burn off.

GROWING METHOD

Planting   Grow carrots throughout most of the year in subtropical regions, but avoid sowing at the height of summer. Sow mid-spring to end of summer in warm zones, and spring to end of summer in cold regions. Seeds take up to three weeks to germinate. First prepare furrows or drills 10 in apart and sow seeds 1/4 in deep. Cover with seed raising mix and water lightly. When seedlings are about 2 in high, thin out to 3/4 in apart. When remaining seedlings reach 6 in, thin out again to 2 in apart. The discarded seedlings can now be eaten as "baby" carrots.

Watering   Important for growing good quality carrots. Small amounts only are required during the first eight weeks of seedling growth. This forces a desirable downwards growth of the roots. Water heavily only if soil dries out as the crop matures. Too much water induces root crack.

Fertilizing   Do not overfertilize garden beds. Those that have been heavily manured the previous season work best, which is something to keep in mind when rotating crops. If necessary, dig in a complete fertilizer NPK 6:6:6 a week before sowing at a rate of 4 oz per square yard. Too much nitrogen leads to excessive leaf growth and poor colored roots.

Problems   Carrot aphids should be controlled with a registered pesticide. Root nematodes cause leaves to curl and turn deep red or yellow if not treated. Diseased plants should be immediately pulled out and burned and the garden bed fumigated.

HARVESTING

Picking   The good thing about carrots is they can be harvested at whatever size you want them. Full maturity is reached approximately 4 months after planting, depending on variety and area. To harvest, use a garden fork and lift carrots gently out of the ground when soil is moist to prevent the roots from snapping.

CAULIFLOWER

Brassica oleracea var. *botrytis*

ALTHOUGH SOME COOKS *overlook the cauliflower, it is an enduringly popular vegetable. Many varieties are now available.*

FEATURES

Grown as an annual, this plant has a single stalk supporting a solid head made up of a collection of edible flower buds. Heads can be white, green or purple, depending upon which variety of cauliflower is grown. Both quick and late maturing types are available. Cauliflowers are not suited to container growing. "Mini"-sized varieties are now on the market and require only half the growing space of the larger cauliflowers.

CONDITIONS

Climate   Cauliflowers can be grown in most climates but like most brassicas they do best in cooler areas, needing lower temperatures for the flower heads to form.

Aspect   Need protection from both full sunlight and frosts or maturing heads will discolor.

Cultivation   Cauliflowers have large rooting systems and are not suited to container growing. As cauliflowers are heavy feeders, garden beds need to be well fertilized with manure and other organic matter, and the plants fed frequently. The color of white cauliflowers is preserved by blanching or protection from sunlight. While the head is quite small, large leaves are tied together and placed over it. These are replaced as the head grows larger.

GROWING METHOD

Planting   Sow from spring to summer in all areas to establish advanced plants before winter sets in. Sow seeds ¼ in deep in outdoor beds in rows 2 in apart. Use a number of varieties with differing maturing dates so as to extend the harvest season. Seedlings take about 6 weeks to appear and are ready for transplanting when around 4–6 in high. Space at least 24 in apart. Transplant only in cool weather.

Watering   Keep soil moist and air humid around maturing plants to assist head development, but avoid watering directly over the head so as to avoid damage. The head may also need protection from heavy rainfalls.

Fertilizing   As these plants do not like acid soils, 3 to 4 weeks before planting apply 7 oz dolomite and 3½ oz fertilizer NPK 5:6:4 per square yard. Lime also assists in the taking up of the trace element molybdenum by the plant. Side dressings of the same fertilizer can be applied 4 weeks after transplanting seedlings. Cauliflowers will take more manuring and fertilizers than other members of the *Brassica* genus. Dressings of urea will promote growth if applied when heads are starting to form.

Problems   Caterpillars of white cabbage moth and aphids are a problem in warmer zones. Treat with an appropriate organic or commercial pesticide. Yellowing and withering of leaves is due to magnesium or molybdenum trace element deficiency. Water seedlings with a solution of 1 oz sodium molybdate dissolved in 5 quarts water.

HARVESTING

Picking   Harvest 4–5 months after planting. Remove heads when about 8 in wide by cutting before they discolor and lose their crisp firmness. Leaves can be used as a vegetable.

CELERY

Apium graveolens

THE BRANCHING STEMS *of a single celery plant allow the outside stalks to be broken off as needed, leaving the plant intact.*

FEATURES

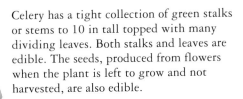

Celery has a tight collection of green stalks or stems to 10 in tall topped with many dividing leaves. Both stalks and leaves are edible. The seeds, produced from flowers when the plant is left to grow and not harvested, are also edible.

CONDITIONS

Climate
Prefers mild to cool weather. Very cold weather will inhibit growth. Seedlings are sensitive to temperatures below 55°F. Grow from midsummer to autumn in warm areas. Tolerates light shade and wet weather.

Aspect Cultivation
Soil needs neutral to alkaline pH level. Liming will reduce acidity. Prepare soil with animal manure and compost and an addition of complete fertilizer. Water and side dress biweekly and keep weed-free. For white celery, cover maturing stalks with opaque coverings fixed with elastic bands or mound with soil as they grow with leaves left exposed to sunlight. Protect from snails and slugs under covers and aerate stalks for short periods every couple of weeks.

GROWING METHOD

Planting
Plant in spring to summer in cool areas, winter through to summer in warm zones and summer though to autumn in tropical areas. In temperatures above 55°F plant seed directly into open beds. Seed viability is often poor, so use fresh seeds for new plantings, sown 1/10 in deep in seed beds. Keep well watered throughout the 2–3 week germination period. After this thin seedlings out when 4–6 in high and plant in garden. Position 10 in between plants and in trenches 4 in deep, with 16–18 in between rows. Mound soil around young plants with roots well covered and thoroughly watered in.

Watering
Celery requires a great deal of water from seed to maturity, with daily watering being needed during hot dry weather. Lack of water leads to slow growth and stringy, tasteless stalks. As it is a shallow rooting plant constant watering may result in essential nutrients being leached from the soil. This means a continual fertilizing program is necessary to ensure constant and healthy growth.

Fertilizing
Enrich beds with complete fertilizer NPK 5:6:6, 7 oz per square yard. Apply regular and frequent side dressings of fertilizer throughout the growing period. Occasional dressings of sulfate of ammonia, 1 oz per square yard, will assist growth.

Problems
A fungal disease known as leaf spot or septoria may affect this plant, producing dead spots on leaves. Control by the use of an appropriate fungicide spray. This disease is spread by infected seeds, and one way of controlling it is by heating seeds to 135°F in a pan of water for 10 minutes. Magnesium and calcium deficiency in soil also increases risk of disease.

HARVESTING

Picking
Celery matures 4–5 months from planting. Cut whole plant at ground level before seed stalks appear, or do occasional harvesting by breaking off outside stems as needed.

CHAYOTE

Sechium edule

THE CHAYOTE VINE *likes lots of room to grow. Support it on a fence at the back of the garden, or train it over a shed or a wall. Strong, coiled tendrils assist its climbing.*

THE PEAR-SHAPED *fruit of the chayote has greenish-white, bland-tasting flesh.*

FEATURES

Chayote, also known as choko, has various names. The green-white fruit, looking rather like a flattened pear, is borne on large, vigorous, rambling vines. It needs considerable support and produces both male and female flowers. Leaves are large and hairy to the touch. This plant requires plenty of space but is easy to grow and relatively trouble free.

CONDITIONS

Climate   Best suited to subtropical and warmer areas of temperate zones. Severe frosts will kill the vine, but in cooler areas the vine will die down over winter with new growth in spring.

Aspect   Prefers to be positioned in warm sunny spots against a wall. During cool to cold snaps it is possible for chayote to be grown in a pot. It can then be brought inside and replanted out when the weather warms up.

Cultivation   A warm 6-month growing season is needed for fruit to reach maturity. Dig in a lot of organic matter and fertilizer before planting. Beds need to be well drained and built up if necessary. Keep weeds down during growing period. After harvesting and before winter sets in, cut vine back to 3 or 4 shoots and mulch heavily to protect the tuberous root system.

GROWING METHOD

Planting   Select a mature chayote showing signs of a germinating seed from your grocer. During early spring in warm climates and in autumn through to spring in tropical zones, plant the whole chayote 4 in deep in damp soil at an angle, with the broad or shooting end downwards and the other end showing just above soil level. Plant near a fence or other strong supporting structure. To ensure success, plant 2 or 3 plants a yard apart.

Watering   Requires plenty of water to keep vine growing, especially during late summer harvest period.

Fertilizing   Several weeks before planting, prepare bed with complete fertilizer NPK 5:6:4, 7 oz per square yard. Side dress with same fertilizer, 3½ oz per square yard, in midsummer. During second year of growth fertilize again around the new shoots during early spring.

Problems   Relatively free from pests and diseases. Aphids and pumpkin beetle may be a problem. Spray or dust with appropriate insecticide.

HARVESTING

Picking   Two crops can be harvested in tropical zones in spring to early summer, and in summer in warm areas. The fruit is at its best when light green in color and about 2 in long. Large fruit, sometimes with prickly spines on the skin, is both coarse in texture and lacking in flavor when cooked.

CHILIES & PEPPERS

Capsicum annuum

THESE PEPPERS *are ready to be picked. If left on the vine, their color will gradually turn to red and the flesh will sweeten.*

PEPPERS AND CHILIES *produce fruit of many different colors and shapes. Flavors range from mild and sweet to pungent and fiery.*

FEATURES

Peppers are perennials but often grown as annual crops. The pepper plant grows to an erect, compact bush and has a reasonably deep root system. Chilies, which are small, often colorful, peppers, produce green or purple fruit which changes to bright red, yellow or orange at maturity.

Peppers may be roundish or long, flat and twisted and green, red, yellow to white, or purple to dark chocolate. Peppers and chilies do well in the open garden, and are excellent and particularly decorative when grown in containers. The chili is notable for its fiery-hotness, while the pepper has a delicate, rather sweet, mild flavor.

CONDITIONS

Climate
Hot peppers will tolerate hotter climates than sweet peppers, but overall peppers are best grown as warm season plants, growing right throughout the year in tropical and subtropical regions. In temperate zones the season is shorter, fruiting only over the summer months. Over winter, die-back may occur but plants shoot again in spring revealing the true perennial nature of the plant.

Aspect
Need plenty of warmth and full sun (average soil temperatures between 60–86°F) and are not suitable for growing in frost-prone areas. Ideal for container growing indoors with access to sunlight, or on verandahs or courtyards where they can be quite decorative. Chilies need protection from strong winds.

Cultivation
As a precaution before planting peppers, prepare garden beds with organic matter and added fertilizer, although peppers will grow in most soils. Once flowering has commenced, monthly side dressings of fertilizer will promote fruiting. Mature plants may need supporting if they are grown in wind-prone areas.

When growing chilies, prepare the garden beds with lots of nitrogenous organic matter. This will cut down the need to over-fertilize with chemical substitutes which could lead to large leafy plants, but few chilies. The fruit will usually develop after insect pollination of the flowers. Crops should be rotated over several seasons—do not plant them where vegetables from the same family, such as eggplants or tomatoes, have been previously grown.

GROWING METHOD

Planting   Sow during spring to early summer in temperate and cooler regions; all year round, but mainly in autumn, in warmer tropical and subtropical zones. Sow seeds 8–10 weeks before planting out. Seedlings are best in the open garden, especially in colder regions, because of the short growing period. In warm climates, direct seeding into garden beds is possible. Plant successively every 2 months to give a continuous crop. Seedlings should be about 6 in tall when planted out, spaced 20 in apart in rows 24 in apart.

Fertilizing   Apply basal fertilizer dressing NPK 5:6:4 to beds a week before planting. Fertilizer can be laid in furrows 6 in deep and 4 in wide, then covered by refilling with soil to ground level. After flowering and when fruit has set, apply monthly applications of urea, ½ oz to a yard row, applied as a band 6 in from the plant and watered in straight away. Do not overfertilize as too much nitrogen leads to large plants but no fruit.

Watering   Keep plants watered so that soil is evenly moist to prevent flower drop. Too much watering, however, can lead to waterlogging and cold soils. If growing in containers, carefully monitor moisture levels.

Problems   Aphids, fruit fly and cutworm are the main pests. Aphids should be washed off the plant with vigorous hosing or, alternatively, may be sprayed with the appropriate chemical insecticides. Sprays also control fruit fly and cutworm. Watch out for powdery mildew in climates that are hot and humid. Crop rotation or planting in different beds each year is advisable if soil-borne diseases such as wilting occur. Do not plant peppers where vegetables from the same family, for example eggplants or tomatoes, have been previously grown.

HARVESTING

Picking   Peppers and chilies take 3–4 months to mature. Peppers are sweeter if left to ripen on vine until turning red with the flesh still firm to touch. Cut to remove, leaving a little brittle stem attached to fruit. Chilies may be picked at any color stage but will be hotter if left to ripen fully.

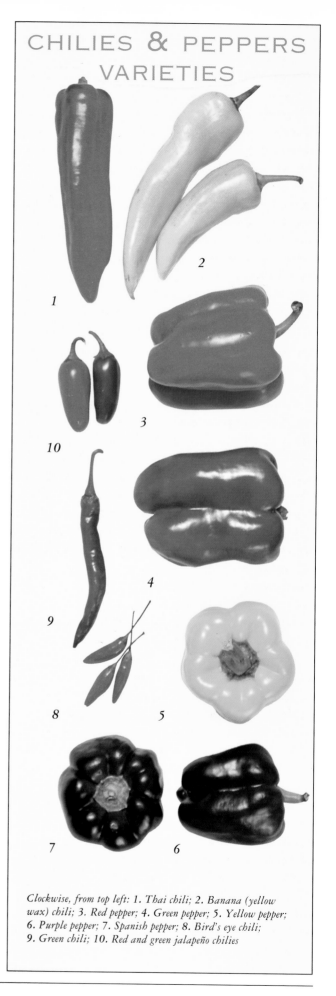

CHILIES & PEPPERS VARIETIES

Clockwise, from top left: 1. Thai chili; 2. Banana (yellow wax) chili; 3. Red pepper; 4. Green pepper; 5. Yellow pepper; 6. Purple pepper; 7. Spanish pepper; 8. Bird's eye chili; 9. Green chili; 10. Red and green jalapeño chilies

CHINESE BROCCOLI

Brassica oleracea var. alboglabra

THE BROAD LEAVES *of the Chinese broccoli, as well as its thick stem, are edible. The plant can also be grown in containers.*

FEATURES

Chinese broccoli is known by various names such as gai lun or kailan and is often used in Asian cooking. This is a stout leafy plant growing to around 18 in. It has thick, crisp leaves which are blue-green to gray with a waxy look. The leaves have different shapes and sizes, depending on the variety. The plant has medium-sized attractive white or yellow flowers. Chinese broccoli is cultivated as a vegetable for its chunky edible ¼–¾ in stem. It is only suitable for container growing if young plants are to be harvested. Older plants need to be grown in the garden. It has a small, shallow rooting system.

CONDITIONS

Climate Can be successfully grown in all climatic zones, even tolerating frosts once past the seedling stage.

Aspect Chinese broccoli does best in a sunny position in fertile, well-drained beds. Needs to be protected from strong winds which may "lift" and move the plant as a result of its shallow rooting system.

Cultivation Prepare the soil with organic material such as compost and animal and poultry manure. In addition, provide extra nitrogen supplements in liquid fertilizers, especially if the soil is sandy. For plants exposed to windy conditions, firm soil up around roots for strength and protection. This is a vigorous-growing plant maturing in around 12–14 weeks. Secondary shoots will appear after main flowering shoot is cut. This method of cultivation ensures three crops.

GROWING METHOD

Planting Sow in all areas from late spring through summer to early autumn, with midsummer sowings producing the heaviest yields. If harvesting young plants, scatter seed direct into garden or a large container, thinning later to 6 in apart. For plants that are left to mature and with a longer harvest period, sow seeds direct into garden position but space 12 in apart. Plant out when 3 in tall.

Watering As a leafy crop, it grows quickly so keep soil moist and water frequently.

Fertilizing Dig in 2 lb poultry manure and 3½ oz complete fertilizer NPK 6:6:6 per square yard. Side dressings of sulfate of ammonia through the growing season or weekly applications of liquid seaweed aid growth.

Problems Susceptible to downy mildew. Treat with appropriate fungicide. Plant leaves also give cover to slugs and caterpillars. Spray or dust for protection.

HARVESTING

Picking If plant is left to mature, it can be harvested over a long period. Cut the shoots or stems when approximately 6 in long and before the flowers open. Harvest frequently in hot climates to prevent plant bolting and shoots becoming tough. Alternatively, the whole plant can be harvested while quite young, usually about 6 weeks after sowing.

CHINESE CABBAGE

Brassica rapa var. *pekinensis*

CHINESE CABBAGE, with its sweet, lettuce-like flavor, is becoming increasingly popular as a salad vegetable.

FEATURES

Chinese cabbage has many names including celery cabbage and wong bok. It has wide, thick, crisp leaves with a prominent, broad-based midrib. The upright heads are either loose or tight, depending on variety. Leaf color varies between dark and light green with inner leaves having a creamy-white color. Plant grows to 12–18 in. The flavor ranges from mustardy to sweet and is rather like lettuce. It is not suitable for containers.

CONDITIONS

Climate Best in cool temperatures between 55–68°F. Tropical varieties have also been developed.

Aspect Prefers open sunny position but tolerates part shade. Shelter from cold winds and frost.

Cultivation Deep, well-drained soils, high in organic matter will retain soil moisture and lessen soil compaction. Avoid both light and heavy soils and lime if necessary so that pH range is between 6.5 and 7. Rapid growth results from regular fertilizing and watering. Slow growth leads to plant going to seed. Bolts during hot dry weather and where days are long. Select varieties to suit local conditions. Mulch heavily to retain soil moisture and ward off bacterial rot. Bind heads as they reach maturity for tender white inner leaves.

GROWING METHOD

Planting Plant all year round in tropical and subtropical climates. Plant winter through spring in warm zones and spring through summer in cold regions. Whatever the local conditions, plant to avoid vegetable reaching maturity in periods of frost in frost-prone areas. Sow seeds 1/5 in deep and in clumps along the row so that when the seedlings are thinned out plants are 12–16 in apart. For irrigation purposes, have 14–16 in of space between rows. It is best to plant seeds direct into the garden as seedlings do not transplant very well. Seedlings will emerge 1–2 weeks after planting.

Watering Requires a great deal of watering to encourage fast growth. Irrigation between beds helps keep water off leaves and reduces the risk of fungal diseases.

Fertilizing Dig in a complete fertilizer NPK 5:6:4 at a rate of 3 1/2 oz per square yard a week before planting. A month after planting spread small amounts of the same fertilizer around the planting area and water in immediately. When cabbages start to form heads, apply a light dressing of urea at a rate of 1/2 oz per square yard.

Problems Prone to soil diseases such as club root and bacterial soft rot. Protect the crop by liming and rotating with an unrelated crop several times over a few years. Dust or spray against caterpillars and aphids.

HARVESTING

Picking This quick-growing crop matures in 2–3 months and should be cropped when weather is dry. Timing is essential as the appearance of seed stalks will cause the heads to split. To avoid splitting the heads cut them when they feel solid. When ready the heads should be cut just above soil level.

CHINESE SPINACH

Amaranthus tricolor

THE VARIEGATED *leaves of Chinese spinach are highly nutritious; the flavor is quite different from that of other spinach varieties.*

FEATURES

Amaranths are a very large group of plants, this species being a colorful leafy variety cultivated for its nutritional value. An erect, branching annual it grows to 3 ft or more under ideal conditions. Soft textured leaves can grow to 6 in. The leaves are pointed or round and light to dark green with red to purple markings on both leaves and stems. Flavor is somewhat like that of an artichoke, taking on a "hot" taste in older plants. It grows well in containers where the decorative leaves look most attractive.

CONDITIONS

Climate Best grown in hot climates above 68°F. Will grow under cover where temperatures are controlled.

Aspect Prefers sunny position sheltered from winds in cool areas. Tolerates partial shade in hot areas.

Cultivation Grows in light, sandy to heavy soils which are well drained. Soil must, however, be quite fertile and preferably slightly acidic. Dig in plenty of organic material in the form of compost, decayed animal and poultry manures. If the beds are well prepared in this way there will be little need for chemical fertilizers. Plant may bolt if left to dry out in hot weather and if so, remove any flowers and seed heads that appear.

GROWING METHOD

Planting Plant seeds in spring and summer in warm and tropical areas. Sow seed direct into garden beds, when soil warms to around 68°F. Successive sowings biweekly will give a longer harvest period. The seeds are very small and should be sown after first mixing with coarse wet sand, which is then set aside in a dark place for one or two days. The sand and seed mixture is then placed in trenches to a depth of 1 in and firmed over. Keep trenches 10 in apart and thin seedlings to 3–4 in apart. Seeds can also be germinated under cover in late spring to early summer. Seedlings appear in 2–3 weeks after seeds are sown and can be transplanted out when about 1 in high and showing 2–3 true leaves. Young growth cuttings may also be taken from lateral shoots which have not yet flowered. Chinese spinach can also be propagated from cuttings which are usually taken from the areas of younger growth or side shoots which have not flowered.

Watering It is essential to keep soil constantly moist for succulent growth.

Fertilizing Feed occasionally with a dressing of nitrogenous liquid.

Problems Damping off of young seedlings causing them to wither and flop is a problem. In warmer climates caterpillars and stem borer may also be a problem. Treat with appropriate sprays.

HARVESTING

Picking Takes 6–8 weeks from sowing to reach cropping stage. There are several ways to harvest. Tips of larger plants can be picked while quite young or the whole plant may be pulled from the ground roots and all, when approximately 10 in tall. Alternatively cut the mature plant back to 1 in above ground level, leaving some of the stem and a few basal leaves to promote regrowth.

CUCUMBER

Cucumis sativus

CLIMBING CUCUMBERS *need plenty of space and are not suitable for containers. This variety, with its attractive bright yellow flowers, has been placed at the back of the garden against a supporting wire fence. Bush varieties, taking up less space, are better for smaller gardens.*

FEATURES

Bush and vine varieties of cucumber are available with the former being suited to container growing. Comes in many forms, including long and short green varieties and the round and whitish apple cucumber. An easily digestible, burpless, thin-skinned variety is now very popular.

CONDITIONS

Climate   Best in warm zones. Grows in most areas with a shorter growing season in cold areas.

Aspect   Prefers warm garden beds with soils above 60°F. Train vine varieties up a trellis to save space and for cleaner, better formed fruit.

Culivation   Prepare beds with compost and animal manures. Add lime to acidic soils or in areas of high rainfall to prevent molybdenum trace element deficiency which is recognized by mottling and curling of leaves. Spray young plants with a solution of sodium molybdate, ⅕ oz to 5 quarts water, to rectify this deficiency. Mulch soil to avoid compaction and to compensate for heavy watering cycle.

GROWING METHOD

Planting   Plant late spring through to summer in cold climates, spring through to summer in warm zones, and from midwinter to mid-autumn in tropical and subtropical areas. Sow seed directly into bed to a depth of ⅔ in as cucumber does not transplant well. Sow seeds 20 in apart and in rows 1 yard apart. Or sow several seeds in shallow craters spaced 20 in apart. When seeds germinate the seedings may be culled to two or three healthy seedlings.

Watering   Cucumbers have an extremely high water content so plants need to be watered regularly during the growing cycle. Drooping leaves during the hottest part of the day may occur, but these are not necessarily a sign of water deprivation, but rather a temporary reaction to extreme conditions. Nevertheless, it is essential that soil moisture levels are carefully monitored at all times to ensure that the water supply is sufficient as otherwise the plants will not thrive.

CUCUMBER VARIETIES

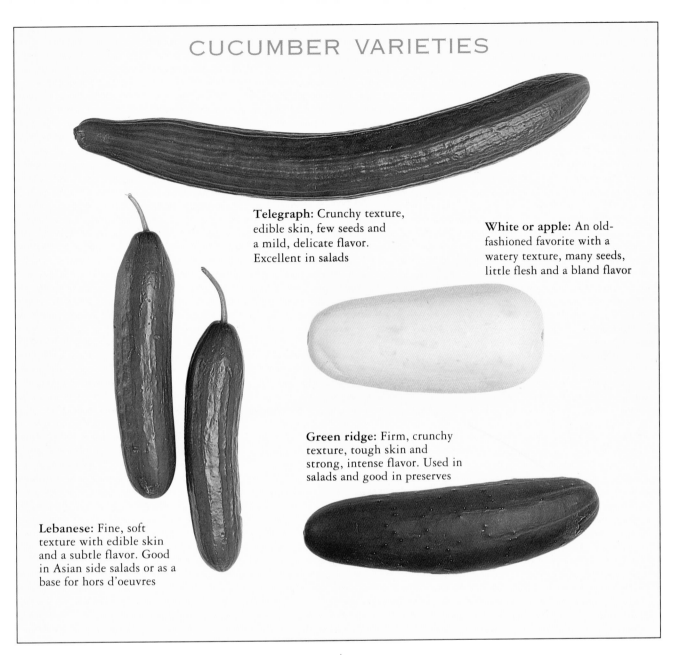

Telegraph: Crunchy texture, edible skin, few seeds and a mild, delicate flavor. Excellent in salads

White or apple: An old-fashioned favorite with a watery texture, many seeds, little flesh and a bland flavor

Green ridge: Firm, crunchy texture, tough skin and strong, intense flavor. Used in salads and good in preserves

Lebanese: Fine, soft texture with edible skin and a subtle flavor. Good in Asian side salads or as a base for hors d'oeuvres

Fertilizing Prepare beds a week ahead with 3½ oz complete fertilizer NPK 5:6:4 per square yard. Make sure fertilizer is well dug in. Proper preparation will result in successful growth through early development. At later stages of growth when the vines start to show signs of vigorous growth, use side dressings of urea, ½ oz per plant, and water in immediately. Repeat this application at regular monthly intervals when vine commences to fruit.

Problems The banded pumpkin beetle will attack foliage and flowers. Treat with sprays containing appropriate insecticide. Aphids and red spider mite will also need spraying if natural predators cannot control any infestations. Powdery mildew is a common disease which discolors leaves. Spraying both upper and lower surfaces with an appropriate fungicide will control both powdery and downy mildew.

HARVESTING

Picking There are optimum times to pick fruit, depending on variety and climate. As a general rule, when the small spiny hairs on the fruit are easily brushed off, the fruit is ripe and ready for harvest. At this stage, the seeds are not large and the taste has not become bitter. It is always best not to let the fruit become old and tough. Frequent harvesting will lead to greater flower production and subsequent fruiting.

EGGPLANT

Solanum melongena

THE MATURING FRUIT ON *this yard high bush of purple eggplant is quite heavy. Plants should be well supported .*

FEATURES

Eggplants grow on small bushes to 5 ft tall with large, coarse, hairy gray-green leaves. The star-shaped flowers are an attractive mauve with yellow centers producing about eight fruit per bush. The fruit varies in shape and size including long and slender or egg-shaped varieties. Color may be dark purple to black or creamy white. There are new small and rounded reddish forms, or even pea-sized green Asian varieties. Eggplants may be grown very successfully in containers.

CONDITIONS

Climate   Definitely a warm climate vegetable, needing temperatures around 77°F and above during the growing season. Eggplant is extremely sensitive to frosts. Extended cool periods will retard growth.

Aspect   Requires full sun, protection from winds and enriched soils.

Cultivation   Eggplant takes 3–4 months to bear fruit. Soil must be well drained and rich in organic matter. Mulch heavily and protect with shade cloths in frost-prone regions. Keep area around plant free of weeds by shallow cultivation.

GROWING METHOD

Planting   Plant spring through autumn in tropical areas, spring through to early summer in temperate zones and during late spring in cool climates. Eggplants need warm soils and warm temperatures to germinate, that is temperatures above 68°F. To ensure a good striking rate, especially in cold areas, sow seeds in small pots or seed boxes at least 8 weeks before transplanting into the open garden during warm weather. Cold soil will shock the plant and set it back considerably. For this reason and because of the fear of soil-borne diseases, many people grow eggplants in containers where conditions are more controllable. Thin out and choose the hardiest seedlings for transplant.

Fertilizing   A few days before planting, dig into top soil 5 oz complete fertilizer NPK 5:6:4 per square yard. Furrow fertilizing in beds to a depth of 6 in and width of 4 in is also recommended. Fill in furrow with soil to cover fertilizer before planting. Side dress with urea, ¾ oz per square yard when first fruit has set.

Watering   Do not overwater as plant is susceptible to root rot. Maintain even moisture and temperature levels in soil by mulching. Watering may be increased as the plant matures.

Problems   Aphids, egg fruit caterpillar and spider mites are main pests. Treat with appropriate sprays. Crop rotation may be necessary to lessen incidence of soil-borne wilt diseases. However, do not grow peppers or tomatoes in succession with eggplants. Leaf spot and fruit rot can be controlled by fungicide sprays.

HARVESTING

Picking   Pick the fruit at full color potential after about 3–4 months and before the seeds harden and turn brown. The skin should be tight, firm and unwrinkled. Over-ripe fruit is coarse and bitter. Cut hard, woody stems with a sharp tool to prevent damage to fruit.

ENDIVE

Cichorium endivia

THE FRILLY LEAVES of *curly endive will taste less bitter if the plant is covered with straw several weeks before harvest.*

FEATURES

This salad vegetable is similar to lettuce but with chewier and more substantial, slightly bitter leaves. There are two frequently grown varieties. Green curly endive has a loose head, finely serrated or frilly leaf edges and white midribs. Batavian endive, or escarole, has broad leaves that are thick, smooth and light green. An unrelated plant is Belgian endive, a young blanched sprout of the chicory family.

CONDITIONS

Climate   Best as a cool season crop, curly endive being the most cold tolerant.

Aspect   Prefers direct or partial sun. In hot weather shade transplanted seedlings, if necessary.

Cultivation   Needs good drainage and soil well worked and manured. Rooting system is shallow so feed close to surface. Dig manure into top 8 in of soil. Prefers neutral to slightly acidic soils, pH range 5–6. Mulch to preserve even soil temperature and moisture levels and keep weeds down. Treat as an annual.

GROWING METHOD

Planting   Sow seeds late summer and early autumn to give a winter crop. In warmer climates sow from autumn to spring. If growing from transplanted seedlings, plant out well before weather gets hot. Hot summers will force plants to bolt and go to seed. Thickly sown seed in containers, harvested when quite young, will produce less bitter endive, but if left to mature in these overcrowded conditions plants will tend to bolt and be more susceptible to disease. Seeds should be sown ¼ in deep in rows 20 in apart in soil that is rich in humus and which has been thoroughly watered beforehand. Germination takes 10–14 days. Later, thin 4-week-old seedlings out to 12 in apart.

Fertilizing   Two weeks before planting prepare bed by digging in 4 lbs poultry manure and 3½ oz complete fertilizer NPK 5:6:6 per square yard of garden bed.

Watering   Water endive regularly to encourage growth and prevent bitterness developing in leaves—it will occur if roots dry out. Overhead sprinklers are not recommended as surplus water becomes trapped inside the endive head resulting in rot.

Problems   Has no serious diseases, but insect pests such as snails, aphids and cutworm can be a problem. Organic gardeners trap snails by placing small containers of stale beer sunk to soil level in the garden. A saucer is ideal for this purpose. Aphids can be washed off by thorough hosing. Plant collars may be used to discourage cutworm.

HARVESTING

Picking   If not harvesting very young leaves, endive will reach maturity in 2–3 months. Cut plant off at soil level. To reduce bitterness in leaves, cover with layers of straw several weeks before harvest. This exclusion of sunlight, or blanching, slows down production of chlorophyll (green coloring) in leaves.

FENNEL

Foeniculum vulgare

THE SWOLLEN *leaf base of the fennel plant forms its stem. It is this part of the plant that is prized for its delicate aniseed flavor. Use the leaves for garnishing.*

FENNEL'S DELICATE, *feathery foliage and yellow flowers make a fine display.*

FEATURES

There are several varieties of this hardy perennial which can grow to 5 ft. This is a lovely plant with attractive feathery leaves. *F. vulgare* var. *dulce* or sweet fennel has a large celery-like stem. *F. vulgare* var. *azoricum* is known as Florence fennel, or finocchio, has a large swollen leaf base and is widely used in cooking. A third variety, much admired for its reddish brown foliage, is *F. vulgare* 'Purpurum' or bronze fennel. The variety now classified as a weed which has taken hold along roadsides everywhere is *F. vulgare*, subspecies *vulgaris*, also known as wild fennel. Green or bronzey feathery leaves on broad petioles branch alternately from the hollow stems. Small yellow flowers clustered in umbels appear in summer and produce oval-shaped, ribbed brown seeds.

CONDITIONS

Climate   Best in hot, dry climates but will grow in practically all climates.

Aspect   Prefers plenty of sun. Plant towards the back of garden where it will be a good backdrop for other plants. The feathery leaves may require tying and support against wind.

Cultivation

Will grow in most soils (pH range of 6.0–7.0 preferred) but it's advisable to dig in plenty of compost and decayed animal manure and have well-drained beds. Applications of lime or dolomite, 3½ oz per square yard, are needed if soil is too acidic. In cooler regions, cut herb back to a hand span above ground level as winter approaches. The swollen leaf bases of Florence fennel are blanched by hilling soil around base of plant to exclude any sunlight.

GROWING METHODS

Planting   Plant seeds quite deeply, around 2 in, in furrows during autumn in tropical and warm zones and during spring in colder regions. Keep the rows 20 in apart and when seedlings appear, thin out to 18 in apart. Pick a permanent position in the garden as the plant will self-sow if left to its own devices. Mature plants may also be lifted during the spring and root cuttings taken and replanted.

Watering   Do not water excessively.

Problems   No specific pests and diseases.

HARVESTING

Picking   Plants take several months to mature. Pick fresh leaves as required. Gather seed heads before they turn brown while still slightly green, and dry in a cool, shady place.

GARLIC

Allium sativum

GARLIC NEEDS *similar growing conditions to its relative the onion. Note the leaf structure which is common to most of the* Allium *genus.*

FEATURES

A bulbous perennial (although usually grown as an annual), garlic has green, curved, flat, spear-like leaves and grows to 24–36 in. Cloves, sheathed in a papery covering, are compacted to form a bulb and cling to a central stem. They have a strong odor and taste. The plant has a central rounded stalk in summer with a large rounded flower head composed of numerous pinkish-white petals. Elephant or Russian garlic *(A. giganteum)* has huge cloves with a few segments to a bulb. It has milder taste than common garlic, a mauve flower head, and grows to 5 ft.

CONDITIONS

Climate As with onions, garlic can be grown in most climates, from protected coastal positions to inland regions. It is frost resistant at all stages.

Aspect Prefers full sun in open position.

Cultivation Soil should be well-drained sandy loam, rich in humus and not too acid, pH around 6.0. With strongly acid soils apply 3½–7 oz ground limestone or dolomite per square yard. Keep weed-free. Left in the ground, the plant will die back in autumn after flowering.

GROWING METHOD

Planting Division of bulb into cloves should take place in early spring. Replant the cloves in spring to summer in warm climates, in winter to spring in tropical areas and in spring in very cold areas. Sow directly into the ground where the plants are to grow 6 in apart in rows and 1½ in deep. Rows should be 12 in apart.

Fertilizing Prepare beds with application of complete fertilizer NPK 5:6:6 at a rate of 5 oz per square yard. Do not provide nitrogen in the form of animal manure or bone meal fertilizer unless organic matter is completely broken down. Apply several months before sowing if using organic matter.

Watering Keep soil damp but not overwet. Be sparing with watering as bulbs mature, making sure to get rid of excess moisture as otherwise garlic will not store satisfactorily once it has been harvested.

Problems Garlic has practically no problems as the strong oils and chemicals in its foliage repel insects and also have antiseptic properties which deter bacteria and fungal diseases. Keep plants well spaced to reduce humidity which can affect the plant, especially in coastal areas. Garlic is useful as a companion plant for fruit trees, tomatoes and roses. The strong secretions of sulfur from garlic are thought to improve the scent of roses. Garlic spray is very useful as a deterrent to pests such as aphids, cabbage worm, caterpillars, spiders and ants.

HARVESTING

Picking The best time to harvest the underground bulb is in summer when the flower dies and the leaves begin to turn yellow. Alternatively, harvest when plant is in full bloom. To do this bend stems in half and leave for 8–10 days. At the end of this period ease bulbs out of the ground with a fork taking care not to damage the bulbs.

GINGER
Zingiber officinale

ABOVE GROUND, *the ginger plant resembles bamboo with its tapering leaves. The root is an indispensable flavoring for Asian food.*

FEATURES

Ginger is an underground stem or rhizome with several knobbly branches. The adult plant looks something like bamboo, growing to 3 ft high with narrow pointed leaves about 9 in long and small flowers, yellow to yellow-green with touches of purple. The rhizome skin is light beige to tan, and the edible flesh pale gold to cream. Ginger has its own particular hot flavor varying from sweet to dry and is very aromatic. Other members of the ginger family include the spices turmeric, galangal and cardamom.

CONDITIONS

Climate   Grows best mainly in tropical and subtropical areas where temperatures are at least 77°F and high rainfalls and high humidity are common. It will also grow in temperate zones with hot summers. Frost-prone climates are not suitable. Container growing under controlled climatic conditions is possible.

Aspect   Prefers sun to partial shade in rich, loamy soils with good drainage. Protect from winds.

Cultivation   Needs little cultivation during growth. Well-prepared garden beds that contain organic matter such as compost and manures to make them water retentive are essential, and these must be well drained to cope with the heavy watering program. Mulching with straw will help to achieve this result. If using containers, dry plant off in winter and replant in spring. Ginger requires spotlessly clean cultivation as once soil diseases exist they are hard to eradicate. Crop rotation over 2–5 years is recommended.

GROWING METHOD

Planting   Plant in spring in warm areas and in winter in tropical zones. Ginger is propagated by detaching part of the original stem, usually a young budding rhizome, which is then cultivated into a complete plant. Dig garden trenches 8 in deep and 10 in wide and incorporate animal manure along bottom of trench. Place rhizomes 6 in apart and with buds pointing upwards. Cover with 4 in of a compost and soil mix and water in. Cover trench with a mulch of straw. If planting in a container, place a 2 in piece of rhizome with good buds horizontally and about 2 in deep in a small pot containing equal parts sand, vermiculite, compost and good garden loam. Move to a larger pot as plant grows.

Fertilizing   Do not overfertilize as leaves will grow at expense of rhizome. Container grown ginger may need mild fertilizer once a month.

Watering Problems   Requires plenty of water during growth. Like any rhizome-type vegetable, ginger is affected by soil diseases. Bacterial wilt may cause yellowing of leaves, followed by the rhizome breaking away from the watery stalk. The whole plant should be removed and burnt. Rhizome rot will need to be controlled by soaking seed pieces in an appropriate fungicidal solution. Sterilize any equipment used. Bacterial soft rot is another disease that requires chemical control.

HARVESTING

Picking   There are several ways to harvest ginger. Harvest young ginger within 3–4 months of planting while still green. Use young 3 in shoots to flavor vinegars. Harvest mature rhizomes after nine months when the leaves have died. The rhizome skin will be hard and the flesh will be firm. Long growth periods result in a more fibrous rhizome.

JERUSALEM ARTICHOKE

Helianthus tuberosus

THE JERUSALEM ARTICHOKE'S *distinctive, sweet flavor is not to everyone's taste. In some places it is only grown as food for animals.*

FEATURES

A very hardy perennial belonging to the sunflower family, this has edible tubers resembling young, gnarled potatoes. Rather sweet to taste, Jerusalem artichokes can be cooked in much the same way as potatoes: roasted, boiled or pureed in soups. It is not related to the globe artichoke. Above ground the plant can grow to 8 ft and produces attractive dark-centered yellow flowers with small seeds.

CONDITIONS

Climate   Most areas are suitable. Care needs to be taken during very cold winters or in frosts.

Aspect   Prefers dry, sunny to semi-shaded locations. The plants will require staking if conditions are windy.

Cultivation   Needs little attention throughout the growth period, but bigger tubers will result if the garden bed is well prepared before planting. Dig in plenty of organic matter and use complete fertilizer, and add a little lime just before planting. Be sparing when watering. The young shoots are at their most vulnerable in summer, so guard carefully against snails and slugs. To improve quality nip out flower heads at bud stage. At beginning of winter and just before harvest, the tall flower stems should be cut off close to the ground. In cold climates cover with mulch to keep an even soil temperature.

GROWING METHOD

Planting   Plant late winter to mid-spring in cool regions, midwinter in warm areas and winter through to mid-spring in tropical areas. Although perennial by nature, this vegetable may be planted as an annual, with the mature tubers lifted during winter and then replanted. It has a tendency to take over the garden if the crop is not checked. Late winter to mid-spring are ideal times to plant, using bulbs or tubers from the previous year's crop. Plant 4–6 in down with 24 in between tubers in rows 36 in apart. Shoots should appear within 2–4 weeks.

Fertilizing   These hardy plants require little help, but better yields are obtained if some animal manure is dug into the soil and a complete fertilizer NPK 5:6:4 at 3½ oz per square yard is added before planting.

Watering   Do not overwater. It may be necessary to keep the soil moist during seasonal dry spells.

Problems   Snails and slugs may appear as shoots form. Use commercial preparations to remove them or trap snails in small containers of stale beer sunk to soil level.

HARVESTING

Picking   Harvest after 4–5 months in spring to early summer in most areas.

KOHLRABI

Brassica oleracea Gongylodes group

THIS MATURE PURPLE *kohlrabi has a less sweet flavor than the green variety. The vegetable is much used in Asian cooking.*

FEATURES

Kohl is the German word for cabbage and *rabi* means turnip, and these two words perfectly describe kohlrabi. It is a cabbage-like root producing a swollen white, purple or green, turnip-shaped stem above ground. Circles of edible green leaves grow from the stem. The taste is somewhere between a cabbage and a turnip, not as strong and slightly sweeter than either. This is a favorite vegetable in Asian cuisines.

CONDITIONS

Climate All climates from sub-zero to subtropical are suitable for growing this vegetable.

Aspect Prefers sunny, well-drained beds with cool, moist soil.

Cultivation Soil should be well drained and rich in organic matter. Dig in plenty of well-rotted animal manure. This will help to retain moisture levels in the soil, but do not hill soil around the vegetable as it matures. Aim for a pH range of 6.5–7.5. Kohlrabi has a shallow root system, so keep bed free of weeds by shallow cultivation.

GROWING METHOD

Planting Does not transplant readily, so it is preferable to plant seeds direct into garden beds which should be prepared with fertilizer several weeks before sowing. Thin seedlings to 4 in apart when about 2 in high. Best times to sow are midsummer to autumn in all areas. Early spring sowings are also viable in regions with cooler temperatures.

Fertilizing Apply 7 oz lime or dolomite per square yard along with 3½ oz complete fertilizer NPK 5:6:4. Spread small amounts of the same fertilizer over the garden bed one month after planting and water in immediately. Light side dressings of urea, ⅓ oz per square yard, can be spread around garden bed as the vegetable matures. Do this biweekly, if necessary, and especially if soils are sandy.

Watering Keep top soil evenly moist at all times otherwise the texture of the vegetable will turn towards woodiness.

Problems Common pests are the same as those that attack cabbages such as caterpillars of the cabbage moth, white butterfly and center grub. Early spraying with an appropriate pesticide is recommended every two weeks from seedling stage onwards. Downy mildew is a fungal disease which attacks seedlings. Unless it is checked, leaves turn yellow and shrivel and plant dies. Spray with a registered fungicide. Yellowing of leaves on older plants may also indicate a magnesium deficiency in soil. Water around plants with a solution of 1 oz magnesium sulfate (Epsom salts) in 5 quarts of water.

HARVESTING

Picking Growing season is short, around 8–10 weeks. Always aim to harvest during cool weather when the vegetable has reached 2–3 in in diameter. Kohlrabi has a tendency to bolt in cooler areas where growing season temperatures fall below 66°F.

LEEK

Allium ampeloprasum Porrum group

THE WHITE UNDERGROUND *stem of the leek is just visible here. Leeks will have more flavor if harvested while still young.*

FEATURES

A relative of the onion, this vegetable has a long white underground stem, slightly bulbous at the root end. Green, strap-like leaves protrude above-ground. Most leeks are left to grow to the fully mature state but are much tastier if harvested earlier. The flesh is thick and mildly onion-flavored.

CONDITIONS

Climate Best grown in cool weather in temperatures below 77°F. Growth slower in warm climates.

Aspect Prefers full sun.

Cultivation Fertilize regularly and keep weeds down. Blanch stems by excluding sunlight as plant grows. Lay seedlings into a trench 8 in deep. Hill dry soil around developing stem. In flat beds heap soil around base of young leek, cover stem with newspaper and pile dry soil up around it. Add soil as leek grows. A newspaper collar will protect leaves from soil.

GROWING METHOD

Planting Plant seeds in seed-raising trays spring to autumn in cool climates, in late summer and autumn in warm and tropical regions. In areas where winters are mild, seeds can be planted directly into the garden during late summer. Garden beds may need to be raised to allow for hilling. Transplant when seedlings reach pencil thickness and are 8–12 in tall. Place 4 in apart in rows 6 in apart. To transplant, make holes 6 in deep, place seedling in with roots touching the bottom of hole but do not fill with soil. Over a period regular watering will gradually deposit soil around the young leek and cover roots. Also remove the top third of leaf structure to reduce water loss and to encourage new root growth. While leeks are a cool season crop, during extreme drops of temperature mulch heavily with straw or pine needles, if available.

Fertilizing Dig in nitrogen rich fertilizer NPK 6:6:6 and large quantities of animal manure and other organic material. Regular monthly applications of urea as a side dressing will speed up the growing process.

Watering Water regularly as moist, fertile soil encourages strong growth.

Problems Very few problems as seldom affected by specific pests and diseases. If onion thrips show up, remove them by hosing.

HARVESTING

Picking Leeks take a long time to produce large stems. The growing season takes about 4–5 months from seed stage and 3 months for seedlings. The younger they are the tastier and sweeter the flesh. If you want to harvest when the stems are thick remove top half of leaves in midsummer. Harvest only as you need them but before any frosts set in. The best way to pick is to pull the complete plant from the ground lengthwise.

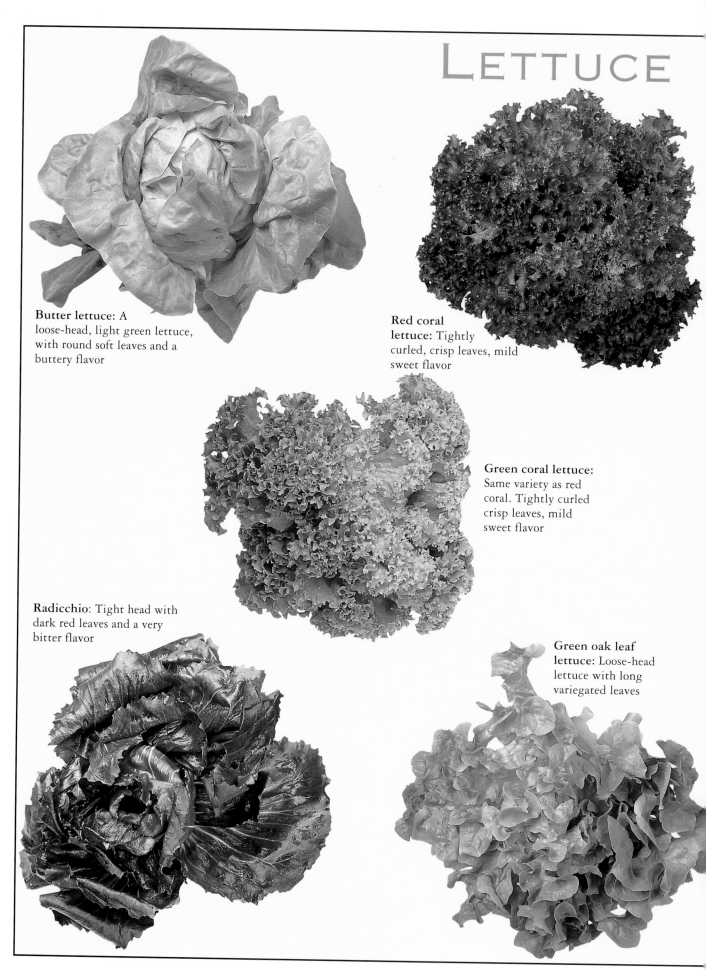

Butter lettuce: A loose-head, light green lettuce, with round soft leaves and a buttery flavor

Red coral lettuce: Tightly curled, crisp leaves, mild sweet flavor

Green coral lettuce: Same variety as red coral. Tightly curled crisp leaves, mild sweet flavor

Radicchio: Tight head with dark red leaves and a very bitter flavor

Green oak leaf lettuce: Loose-head lettuce with long variegated leaves

VARIETIES

Cos lettuce (Romaine):
Large, long green heads, with
crisp, succulent and
sweet leaves

Mignonette lettuce:
Red and green leaves with
a mild, sweet flavor

Iceberg lettuce: Large
crisp leaves with a sweet,
watery flavor

Red oak leaf lettuce: Same
variety as green oak leaf.
Loose-head lettuce with long
variegated leaves

LETTUCE

Lactuca sativa

RAISED, WELL-DRAINED BEDS *provide a comfortable home for leaf lettuce. Leaves on mature lettuce may be snapped off as needed.*

FEATURES

Lettuce is a cool season crop, often in demand as a salad vegetable during hot months. New varieties to suit all seasons are now available. Lettuce has either compact or loosely arranged leaves forming a light green to reddish-brown head. The common iceberg lettuce is an example of the compacted form but it does not have much flavor. Brown and green mignonette forms also have small compact heads. Butterhead (cabbage) and oak leaf varieties have soft, loose leaves while cos (romaine) has strong rigid leaves and a distinctively elongated head. Loose leaf or any small varieties grow well in containers.

CONDITIONS

Climate   With many different varieties, lettuce can be grown in all climates at any time of the year.

Aspect   Prefer sun to partial shade. Do not like excessively hot beds and in cold climates a protective cloche may be needed.

Cultivation   Prefer non-acidic soils, enriched with decayed animal or poultry manure. Dig in 4 lbs per square yard two weeks ahead of planting. Lime or dolomite, 5 oz per square yard, will help neutralize soil acidity. Beds should be well drained and weeds kept under control. Mulching helps this and also keeps the shallow roots cool.

GROWING METHOD

Planting   Plant year round in all areas. Grow quickly for best results. If a variety is planted out of season it will go to seed, especially in hot weather. Succession sowings early spring to midsummer will ensure a continuous crop. Avoid sowing during very hot weather. Seeds can be raised in containers for later transplanting, but direct sowing into garden beds is preferred. Sow several seeds in a shallow depression 10 in apart and lightly cover with no more than 1/4 in of compost or seed raising mix. Keep soil moist. Thin out to single plants when seedlings 2–3 in tall with rows 12 in apart.

Fertilizing   A week before planting, spread fertilizer NPK 5:6:4 across bed 3 1/2 oz per square yard, and dig in. Side dress twice during the growing cycle with 1/3 oz urea per square yard. Dress after thinning seedlings and later when plant is half-grown. Do not let fertilizer touch leaves. Wash off if necessary.

Watering   Keep shallow rooted plants evenly moist. Overwatering may cause fungal diseases. Lack of water can reduce head size, cause bolting in hot weather and increase bitterness in leaves.

Problems   Aphids appear early and slow plant growth. Control with appropriate sprays. Diseases include sclerotinia rot which develops in wet, shaded conditions. White cottony fungal growth appears around stem at ground level, and needs to be treated with suitable sprays biweekly. Downy mildew and septoria or leaf spot are also treated with sprays. Dead leaves should be burned. The general health of plants is improved by keeping plants well spaced during growing period with access to full sun where the ground is wet and soggy.

HARVESTING

Picking   Lettuces take 8–10 weeks to reach maturity, depending on climate. Pick early when hearts start to form. Loose leaf lettuce are often harvested a few leaves at a time, with mature outer leaves being snapped off when needed.

MARROW SQUASH

Cucurbita

MAKE SURE *you allow plenty of garden space for squash vines to stretch their legs. The vegetable grows to a length of around 12 in.*

FEATURES

Marrow is in fact a type of bush pumpkin or summer squash and is sometimes called button squash or even zucchini. The skin is mostly white and turns slightly yellow when mature. Some, such as Lebanese zucchini, have skin which is quite dark and mottled green. There is little difference in taste between varieties, although texture varies. Squash flowers or blossoms are often eaten along with the immature fruit. Male and female yellow flowers appear on the same vine. Female flowers have short, thick stems showing immature fruit just below petals.

CONDITIONS

Climate   Squash are a warm weather crop, sensitive to cold and frosts. Grows in most areas.

Aspect   Prefers full sun to partial shade in a wide range of soils with good drainage.

Cultivation   Dig in plenty of well-rotted manure and compost several weeks before planting. Keep free of weeds and other decaying matter which might harbor disease. Cultivate lightly without disturbing root structure. Lack of fruit may be due to unsuitable weather or lack of bee activity around flowers—hand-pollination may be necessary.

GROWING METHOD

Planting   Plant seeds all year in hot subtropical climates, in spring in warm zones and in early summer in cool regions. Raise seeds in pots 4–5 weeks ahead of planting out in open garden. Plant seeds $4/5$ in deep in seed-raising mix. Alternatively you may sow direct into soil in final growing position. Place several seeds $1/2$ in deep in wide, hollow, saucer-shaped depressions. The depressions should be 8 in deep, the excavated soil being built or hilled up as a rim around edge of depression. Leave 3 ft of garden space between the "hills." Thin to two or three plants at seedling stage and to one healthy plant when true leaves appear. Remove seedlings by cutting stems at ground level being careful not to disturb root structure. If planting in rows, have a clear 5–7 ft space around each plant.

Fertilizing   Dig in $3^{1}/2$ oz complete fertilizer NPK 5:6:6 just before sowing. Apply side dressings of $1/2$ oz urea per square yard when first fruit has set and water in immediately, but remember too much fertilizer will promote vigorous vine growth at the expense of the vegetables.

Watering   Keep water up to plant, but off the vine stems and foliage. Large leaf structure wilts during hot weather and recovers if soil is kept moist.

Problems   Powdery mildew and bacterial wilt is common. Preventative care is important. Do not handle fragile vines while wet and keep garden clean. Diseases such as viral mosaic are spread by insects. Infected plants should be sprayed on upper and lower leaves or removed altogether from garden. Aphids and pumpkin beetle affecting early growth, especially in spring, should be controlled by spraying.

HARVESTING

Picking   Squash reach maturity in 2–3 months, depending on variety. Harvest before frosts set in and before skin hardens. Fruit is usually about 2 in across.

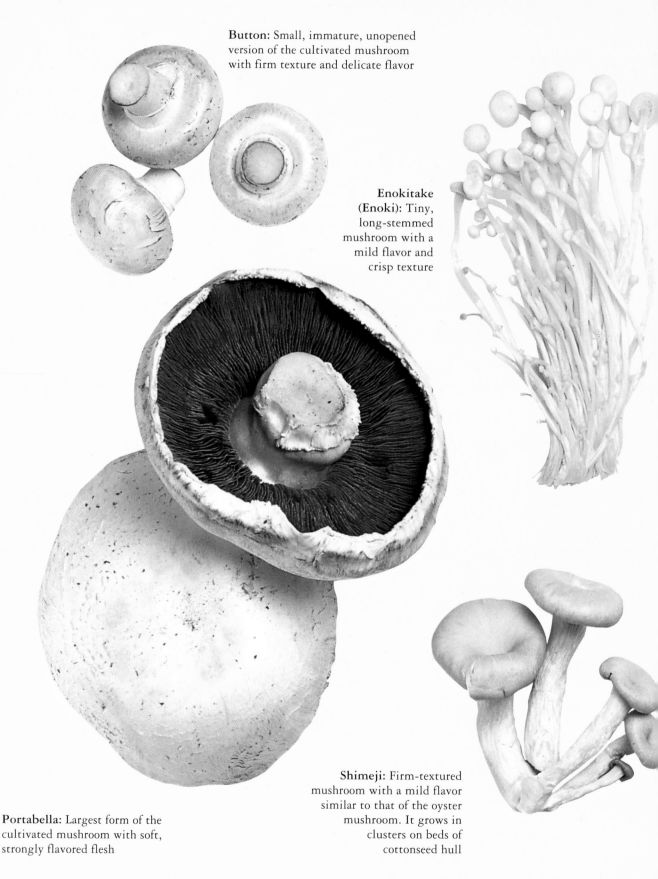

Button: Small, immature, unopened version of the cultivated mushroom with firm texture and delicate flavor

Enokitake (Enoki): Tiny, long-stemmed mushroom with a mild flavor and crisp texture

Shimeji: Firm-textured mushroom with a mild flavor similar to that of the oyster mushroom. It grows in clusters on beds of cottonseed hull

Portabella: Largest form of the cultivated mushroom with soft, strongly flavored flesh

VARIETIES

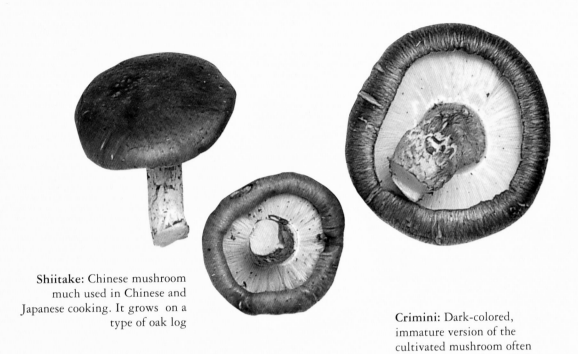

Shiitake: Chinese mushroom much used in Chinese and Japanese cooking. It grows on a type of oak log

Crimini: Dark-colored, immature version of the cultivated mushroom often served raw, sliced, in salads

Oyster mushroom: Pale, fine-textured, creamy-gray mushroom with a flavor reminiscent of oysters

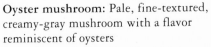

MUSHROOM

Agaricus

THIS ABUNDANT CROP *of mushrooms has its home in a sack of farm compost. A dark spot such as a cellar makes an ideal environment.*

FEATURES

Mushroom is a fungus, the edible part being a spore-producing head which grows upwards from a body of filaments feeding throughout a bed of compost below. Mushrooms have no leaves or chlorophyll and absorb no carbon dioxide from the air. Young mushrooms have a small, white rounded head which opens to a circular cap revealing ridges of pink gills beneath. These turn brown as spores develop between them. There are many poisonous forms of fungi and careful identification is recommended when collecting mushrooms in the field. Many varieties of interesting and unusual mushrooms are now available commercially. These include the pine mushroom with deep yellow to golden gills, the golden enoki, white oyster shimeji and shiitake forms.

CONDITIONS

Climate   As the garden mushroom is mostly grown indoors or under shelter, all climates are suitable.

Aspect   Prefers the dark but will tolerate some light. Direct sunlight is not necessary for growth. The home gardener usually grows mushrooms in dark cupboards or in cellars. Good ventilation is required to remove excess carbon dioxide in the air. Constant, cool to warm temperatures between 54–64°F are recommended.

Cultivation As the mushroom is a fungus and not a true vegetable it gets its food in quite a different way than other vegetables in the garden. After planting in the prescribed manner, grayish colored filaments appear in approximately 1–2 weeks, spreading throughout the compost medium but at the same time growing together to form clumps called mycelium. Pinhead structures, which develop into the mature mushroom, grow from this mycelium forcing their way upwards through the shallow casing.

GROWING METHOD

Planting   Plant all year round in all climates in controlled temperatures. Use sterilized mushroom farm compost, already inoculated with mushroom spawn. Cover with a ¾–1 in layer of commercially available (sterilized) topsoil or peat. This is called the casing. Water lightly just to dampen soil.

Fertilizing Do not fertilize. Initial preparation of the growing medium is satisfactory.

Watering   Keep compost moist but never too wet or soggy. Water two or three times a week.

Problems   No serious diseases but it is a good idea to take precautions. Use commercially available sterilized compost and keep it from getting soggy or wet while growing the crop. Larvae from fly infestations, mushroom mite and nematodes can infest the mycelium and fruiting bodies. Dusting beds with pyrethrum every 2 weeks will help clear this up.

HARVESTING

Picking   Mushrooms mature in about 4 weeks in growth waves called flushes. Button mushrooms are harvested before the cap opens. Mature mushrooms are ripe when the cap opens and gills are exposed. Cut stalks at soil level and pick regularly to encourage further flushes. If, after several flushes, no mushrooms appear within 14–21 days, the bed is exhausted and the planting/cultivation cycle needs to be repeated.

OKRA

Hibiscus esculentus, syn. *Abelmoschus esculentus*

THESE GREEN OKRA PODS *are ready for picking. Before the pods appear, the plant bears attractive, hibiscus-like flowers.*

FEATURES

Also known as gumbo, okra is an annual and a member of the hibiscus family. It is also sometimes known as lady's finger. The large yellow hibiscus-like flowers with red-purplish centers produce edible seed-containing pods which have an unusually high gum content. Because of this, not everyone finds this vegetable to their taste. It is sometimes used as a thickening agent in soups and stews. The pod is green and grows to around 3–4 in. The bush grows to a height of 6 ft with hairy stems and large flattened leaves. It does not grow well in containers.

CONDITIONS

Climate   Best grown in tropical, subtropical and hot temperate climates with long, warm growing seasons.

Aspect   Prefers to be in full sun and requires well-drained soil.

Cultivation   Okra likes moderation in all things such as clay or clay loamy soils that are neither over- nor under-fertilized and of an average moisture level. Beds may need to be raised if there is any danger of rainwater sitting around the crowns. Keep beds reasonably dry and do not cultivate when plants are wet as allergic reactions may set in. Composting will increase the water holding capacity of soil, which is better than having to water frequently. Nitrogen and phosphorus requirements are high. Regularly apply side dressings of liquid fertilizer or urea.

GROWING METHOD

Planting   Sow seeds in spring through to early summer in cool and warm climates. Sow all year round in tropical areas. Seeds can be germinated indoors under controlled conditions and later transplanted, but in most warm climates it is better to plant directly into garden beds. Plant seeds 3/4 in deep and spaced 18 in apart. Flowers take 12–14 weeks to appear.

Fertilizing   Lay a band of complete fertilizer NPK 5:6:4 in furrows 4–6 in deep. Cover with soil and leave a week before planting seed in the furrows. Side feedings, 6 in around plant when pods begin to show, will also help growth. Water feedings in immediately.

Watering   As plant is prone to stem rot, water sparingly around and not over the plant.

Problems   Relatively few problems. Watch out for stem rot in very wet conditions. Crop rotation will prevent build-up of soil diseases. Prevention is advisable so attend to general health of garden, keeping it free of decaying or diseased organic plant matter.

HARVESTING

Picking   Immature pods are picked when 2–3 in long after 3–4 months. If left on the bush too long the pods will become fibrous and tough. Pick daily to lengthen the harvesting period.

ONION

Allium cepa

THE FLESHY UNDERGROUND *bulbs of these onion plants are ready for harvesting. There are several varieties to choose from to suit garden conditions. Plan to have successively maturing crops—spring onions, for example, will be ready quite early.*

FEATURES

This versatile vegetable can be grown in most soils and climates. The edible part is the fleshy bulb which can be white, yellow and brown through to red. Spring onions and scallions (often wrongly called shallots) are grown for their small white bulbs or thin stems and green tops. The common "white" and "brown" onions are late maturing and keep longer than early-maturing varieties.

CONDITIONS

Climate All climates are suitable but it is important to choose varieties to suit local conditions. Planning to suit varieties with different maturing dates and preferred climates is necessary for harvesting over a long period.

Aspect Does not like beds that get too hot and is very temperature-sensitive. Warm weather and direct sunlight promote bulb development, so exposure to full sun is necessary at some stage of growth. Cool weather promotes top growth, so green, early-maturing onions tolerate partial shade.

Cultivation Prefers to be in non-acidic soils around pH 6.0. Prepare the beds well ahead with large amounts of any form of well-decayed organic matter. Control weeds by regular shallow cultivation. When weeding, be particularly careful not to cover the maturing bulbs with soil. The best way to do this is by hilling the soil around the bulbs rather than covering them with soil.

GROWING METHOD

Planting Onions are classified as early, mid-season or late maturing. Plant early varieties in mid to late summer in tropical and subtropical areas, mid to late summer in warm areas, mid to late summer in cold areas. Plant mid-season varieties in autumn in tropical to subtropical areas, autumn to midwinter in warm areas, early winter in cold regions. Plant late-maturing varieties in late autumn to early winter in tropical and subtropical regions, early winter in warm to cold zones. Sow seeds directly in ground or transplant seedlings from seed beds. Seedlings should be 5 in tall when put out. Plant, spaced 3 in apart, in rows 12 in apart.

SPRING ONIONS *have a more delicate flavor than bulb onions. After pulling, leave to dry in the sun before bundling for storage.*

Fertilizing Fertilize before planting and mid-season with dressings of $^3/_4$ oz urea or $1\,^3/_4$ oz sodium sulfate per square yard. Nitrogenous fertilizers in the form of bone meal or animal manures are best, but complete fertilizer NPK 5:6:6, $3\,^1/_2$ oz per square yard, is satisfactory. Avoid using nitrogen as plant approaches maturity as nitrogen promotes foliage at expense of bulbs.

Watering Water regularly and evenly. Lack of water delays growth and leads to bulb splitting.

Problems Onion maggot thrives in fresh organic material in soil, so fertilize with well-decayed material. White stipple on leaves indicates onion thrip. Treat with appropriate spray. Downy mildew is common. Spray biweekly with Manzeb.

HARVESTING

Picking Onions can take over six months to mature, depending on variety. Pull plant from ground and leave to dry in sun, if possible.

ONION VARIETIES

From top: 1. Brown onion; 2. White onion; 3. Red (Spanish) onion; 4. Spring onion (often called shallot); 5. Baby onions; 6. Spring onion

PARSNIP

Pastinaca sativa

PARSNIPS NEED *deeply dug, friable soil to grow well—the roots will fork in hard ground. The leaves resemble those of celery.*

FEATURES

This is a popular garden vegetable because of its high yields, economic growing space and long harvesting period. However, it is not suitable for container growing. Fleshy cream to white underground tap root grows to 8 in with celery-like leaves protruding above ground. The edible root contains a lot of sugar, most of which is lost during cooking, but still giving it a distinctive sweet taste and aroma which is unusual for a vegetable. This is a traditional favorite for some vegetable growers and is a tasty and nutritious addition to any vegetable plot.

CONDITIONS

Climate	Prefers cool weather but grows in all climates.
Aspect	Full sun to partial shade in well-drained organically enriched, deep sandy loams.
Cultivation	Long tap roots will require careful preparation of garden beds by deep digging to allow for growth. Incorporate plenty of well-rotted animal manure to keep soil friable well ahead of planting. Using a garden bed that has been heavily fertilized and mulched for a previous crop is ideal. Avoid deep cultivation as it will damage roots. Hand weed, if necessary. In very hot areas mulch to keep soil cool to stop short root growth.

GROWING METHOD

Planting	Sow seeds in spring through to early summer in cold climates, in midwinter to mid-autumn in temperate zones, and from autumn through winter in tropical and subtropical areas. Seed is not usually viable over long periods so obtain fresh stock each season. Plant seeds 1/5–2/5 in deep in rows 16 in apart in open garden. They will take approximately 5 months to reach maturity. Otherwise raise in seed beds, keeping seed beds damp until seedlings appear. Plant out when seedlings are 5–6 in high and space them 2 in apart.
Fertilizing	Dig in complete fertilizer NPK 6:6:6, 4 oz per square yard, a week before sowing seeds or transplanting seedlings. Do not overfertilize as too much nitrogen leads to heavy leaf growth at the expense of developing roots.
Watering	Give ample water during early stages of growth but ease off as root thickens. Too much water induces root crack. Too little will lead to slow development and even stunting of root.
Problems	No serious diseases, but insects can be a nuisance. Control aphids, which turn leaves curly and reddish-brown, with sprays.

HARVESTING

Picking	Harvest after 4–5 months. Using a garden fork, lift the root gently out of the soil when there is a thickness of approximately 2–3 in across the crown of the vegetable.

PEA

Pisum sativum

THE DWARF PEA'S *bushy habit means it doesn't need trellising, but give it some form of support to keep the plant clear of the ground.*

THIS MINIATURE SUPPORTING *trellis in an interesting cone shape makes an unusual prop for a sugar snap pea.*

FEATURES

Mainly climbing annuals with pretty flowers and green tendrils, the pea is an attractive addition to the home vegetable garden. Some varieties are grown for the seeds contained in the fibrous pod and others for the pods themselves. The most common is the garden pea which is grown for the round green seed in its pod. Snow peas, also known as mange-tout, and sugar snap peas are both varieties of pea that are cultivated for their pods. Edible succulent pods of the sugar snap pea resemble the ordinary pea, with the snow pea being a flatter variety. Leaflets, tasting just like the pea, are sometimes picked and used in salads. Flowers and habit differ but all varieties have the same requirements for successful growth. Dwarf peas are a bushy variety of pea that can be grown without trellising; nevertheless, they need another bush or a form of low support to keep them just clear of the ground. Dwarf peas will crop within 3–4 months of sowing.

CONDITIONS

Climate Most climates are suitable, but plantings should be confined to the cool months of the year for best results. Both flowers and pods are subject to frost damage so avoid harvesting in winter in frost-prone areas.

Aspect Prefers sun to partial shade. In cooler zones shade protection during the hottest part of day may be necessary in summer months.

Cultivation Beds must be well drained and enriched with organic matter. Acid soils need treatment with lime to bring them to a pH level of 6.5. It is also advisable to rotate crops as peas fix nitrogen in the soil through bacterial action in their root nodules and this will affect following pea crops negatively. After harvesting, the whole plant can be dug back into the soil as green manure. For varieties that need it, and most do, trellising permits easier cultivation and harvesting. Lightly cultivate beds to keep weeds down.

GROWING METHOD

Planting Succession planting every 2–3 weeks extends harvest. Sow seeds directly into garden from winter to early spring in cold climates, in autumn through winter in warm zones, and in autumn to early winter in warm subtropical areas. Plant 1 in deep and 2 in apart in cooler climates where rainfall is plentiful, in warmer regions slightly deeper to 2 in. Rows should be 24 in apart. Fill trenches with soil and firm down. Don't water heavily to avoid rotting seeds. Protect seedlings from birds with wire netting.

THE PRETTY WHITE FLOWERS *produced by climbing peas are edible—pick them and use them as a garnish in salads.*

Clockwise from top:
1. Sugar snap pea;
2. Garden pea;
3. Snow pea (mange-tout)

Watering	Water carefully as they need adequate, but not excessive, watering at soil level. Avoid watering over top of mature leaves and flowers.
Fertilizing	Apply complete fertilizer NPK 5:6:4, 4 oz per square yard, to improve the soil fertility.
Problems	Crop rotation is a preventative measure which will inhibit the growth of diseases affecting all parts of the plant structure. These can include the fungal diseases of foot rot, pod and leaf rot, which are prevalent in wet weather. Discoloration of the leaves and pods and the appearance of blackish streaks on the stems indicate disease. After harvesting, remove all vines (healthy or otherwise) and burn them. Don't recycle as green manure. Fungicide dusting of seed before sowing will avert seed rotting and damping-off, especially in areas where winter sowings are in cold soils. Hose aphids off vines or, if badly infected, pick out and destroy all infected foliage. Control grubs which attack pods with carbaryl.

HARVESTING

Picking	Pick when the pods are full, firm, shining, bright green and 2–3 in long. The sugar content will be high at this time. Frequent harvesting from the bottom of the plant prolongs the harvest. Harvest the common pea through winter into early spring in tropical areas, in late summer through to mid-autumn in warm areas and in spring through to late summer in cool zones. Sugar snap peas and snow peas may be harvested autumn through to mid-spring in subtropical zones, autumn and spring in warm zones and in spring through to the end of autumn in cool zones.

POTATO

Solanum tuberosum

GARDEN BEDS *for potatoes should be made up of friable, crumbly soil well prepared with plenty of organic matter. The plants can take up a lot of space in the garden, but they can be grown successfully in containers. The flavor and texture of freshly dug potatoes is worth making space for.*

FEATURES

Although they originated in the high mountain regions of South America, potatoes do not do well in areas of extreme frost or extreme heat. The potato is an underground tuber producing a stem with hairy, tomato-like leaves above ground. Skin range of potatoes is from cream through reddish-brown to dark purple. The flesh is creamy-white to white and either floury or waxy in texture. This is an easy vegetable to cultivate and it grows well in containers.

CONDITIONS

Climate   Potatoes can be grown in all climates. Need a frost-free season of 4–5 months.

Aspect   Grows best in full sun in well-drained fertile soils which should be raised if underlying ground is heavy clay.

Cultivation   Soils must be friable and crumbly and high in organic matter, pH 5.0–5.5. Add lime to soil with care to reduce acidity. Too much lime will increase incidence of scab disease infecting skin, although it may not affect the flesh of the potato. The developing plants should be hilled for support; this will also exclude sunlight from the developing vegetable and protect it from insects. Keep weeds down by shallow cultivation.

GROWING METHOD

Planting   Planting depends on variety used. In general, plant when soils are warm, spring to early summer in cold regions, spring to end of summer in temperate zones, and summer through winter in warm tropical climates. Seed pieces are eyes cut from potato tubers with about 2 oz of flesh attached. Plant in furrows 28 in apart, with seed pieces 14 in apart. Dig furrows to 6 in then lay 2–3½ oz fertiliser along base. Cover with 2 in soil and lay seed pieces on top. Fill with soil and rake topsoil evenly. Alternatively, cover sprouting tubers with 6–10 in of decomposing straw or mulch, then 4 in rich friable soil. Keep moist. Potatoes grow in the straw.

Watering   Water regularly to promote smooth, bigger vegetables. Irrigate along the channels which form between the hilled rows. Reduce the watering just before harvesting when plant tops die off.

Fertilizing   Use a fertilizer high in phosphorus such as NPK 10:7:6.

CAREFULLY LIFT OUT *new potatoes just after the plant has flowered: the delicate skin of the tubers can be easily damaged.*

Problems Potato moth is the most destructive insect pest, attacking exposed tubers in the garden. Covering the vegetable with soil is the best preventative measure that can be taken by the home vegetable grower. Aphids spread mosaic disease and need to be controlled. If the leaf structure is infected treat with appropriate sprays. Blight is a fungus that becomes common in humid weather. When the plant is infected leaves and stems rot, then the tuber flesh becomes spotted and the whole potato finally softens and rots. Spraying with a registered fungicide will prevent development of disease. Another way of dealing with this problem is by the removal and burning of diseased plants.

HARVESTING

Picking "New" or young potatoes can be harvested a month after the plants have flowered and the leaves have turned yellow. There is no need to peel new potatoes as the skin can be easily rubbed off at this stage. "Old" potatoes are those that have been left to mature in the ground and stored until next season. Wait until the plant dies down before lifting. Potatoes grown by straw or mulching methods produce a much cleaner crop.

POTATO VARIETIES

Clockwise from top right: 1. Toolangi delight; 2. Cocktail; 3. Pink eye; 4. Belgian congo; 5. Sebago; 6. Pontiac; 7. New; 8. Bintje; 9. Kipfler

PUMPKIN

Cucurbita

PUMPKINS MATURE ON *fast-growing vines that demand a lot of space to roam. The large flowers that precede the fruit are also edible.*

FEATURES

Small to medium-sized pumpkins belong to the species *C. pepo. C. maxima* produces large fruit, actually a mammoth variety of winter squash, grown for "giant" pumpkin contests. Bush pumpkins and winter squash are classified under this group of cucurbits. They are grown on long, rambling prostrate vines of 20 ft or more. Large (4 in-wide) male and female yellow flowers appear on the same vine. Female flowers have short, thick stems showing immature fruit just below the petals. The fruit has a dry texture and sweet taste, and ranges from yellow to orange-gold. Skins vary from dark green, through whitish-gray to creamy-yellow, depending on variety. The so-called spaghetti squash is a member of the *C. pepo* pumpkin species.

CONDITIONS

Climate   Pumpkin is a warm weather crop, sensitive to cold and frosts. It can be grown in most areas but the colder it gets, the shorter the season.

Aspect   Pumpkin prefers to be grown in full sun to partial shade. Good drainage is essential.

Cultivation   A long growing season is needed so dig in plenty of well-rotted manure and compost several weeks ahead of planting. Keep free of weeds and other decaying matter which might harbor disease. Lightly cultivate, trying not to disturb root structure. If no fruit develops it may be caused by unsuitable weather conditions or lack of bee activity around flowers. Hand-pollination of male and female flowers may be necessary.

GROWING METHOD

Planting   Sow seeds all year round in hot, subtropical climates, throughout spring in warm zones, and confine to early summer in cold regions. Raise seeds in pots 4–5 weeks ahead of planting. Plant seeds ⅘ in deep in seed-raising mix. Alternatively, sow direct into garden soil in final growing position. Place several seeds 1 in deep in wide, hollow saucer-shaped depressions. The depressions should be 8 in deep, the excavated soil being built or hilled up as a rim around edge of depression. Leave 6 ft of garden space between "hills." Thin to 2 or 3 plants at seedling stage and to one plant when true leaves appear. Be careful not to disturb root structure when removing seedlings by cutting stems at ground level. If planting in rows have a clear 4–6 ft space around each plant.

Watering   Keep water up to but off the vine stems and foliage. Large leaf structure wilts during hot weather but recovers if soil is kept moist.

Fertilizing   Dig in 3½ oz complete fertilizer NPK 5:6:6 just before sowing. Side dressings of ¾ oz urea per square yard watered in when first fruit has set can be applied. Too much fertilizer will promote vigorous vine growth at the expense of pumpkin development.

Problems   Powdery mildew and bacterial wilt is common. Preventative care is important. Do not handle fragile vines while wet and keep garden clean. Diseases such as viral mosaic are spread by insects. Infected plants should be sprayed on upper and lower leaves or removed from garden. Aphids and pumpkin beetle affecting early growth, especially in spring, should be controlled by spraying.

HARVESTING

Picking   Maturity is reached in 14–16 weeks and harvest should take place before frosts. Vine dies down leaving hard, dry stalk. Cut free of vine leaving a portion of stem on pumpkin.

Butternut: Bell-shaped pumpkin with delicately flavored, pale orange flesh, and creamy yellow to orange skin which softens with cooking

Japanese: Small to medium, round pumpkin with dull green skin and deep yellow flesh. Although not native to Asia, it is a popular part of Japanese cuisine

Golden nugget: Small, round pumpkins with orange skin and flesh. They cluster around a central stem instead of growing on a long vine

VARIETIES

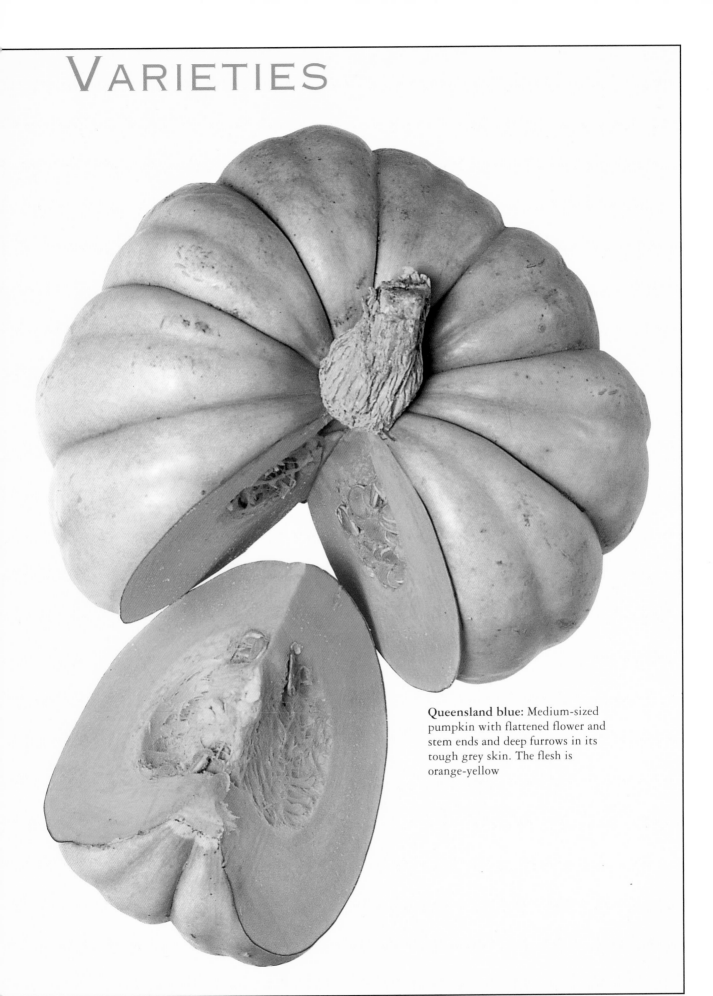

Queensland blue: Medium-sized pumpkin with flattened flower and stem ends and deep furrows in its tough grey skin. The flesh is orange-yellow

RADISH

Raphanus sativus

RADISH COMES *in a variety of shapes. This harvested crop of the red radish shows the small, rounded root form used in salads.*

FEATURES

A round to globular and sometimes cylindrical root vegetable with winter and summer varieties. The longer root form grows to 6 in long and is good for cooking. The smaller, rounder summer radish is usually eaten fresh in salads and is ideal for containers. They are quick growers with sweet flesh which turns bitter and hot if left in the ground too long. The thin skin ranges from red through to white. An easy vegetable for the home gardener to cultivate.

CONDITIONS

Climate   Grows in all climates.
Aspect   Thrives in a moist, shady place where soil has been manured and fertilized for a previous crop. In high summer, needs protection from direct sunlight a few hours of the day.
Cultivation   Needs rich, deep sandy loams with high moisture-holding capacity. Heavily mulch in hot weather. Ready to harvest in 6–8 months, the winter variety taking a little longer. Ideal pH is 6.5. Add lime to soil, if necessary. Do not add manure to established seedlings as this leads to leaf growth at expense of the developing radish. Keep free of weeds by regular cultivation. Has a tendency to bolt or go to seed in hot weather.

GROWING METHOD

Planting   Plant all year round in tropical to subtropical areas; throughout the year except in early winter in warm temperate zones; in spring, summer and early autumn in colder regions. Successive sowings every two or three weeks ensures a continuous crop. Because it is quick growing, radish can be planted in alternate rows with slow growing vegetables such as lettuce. Plant seed directly into the soil ¼ in deep, 2 in apart, and in rows 6 in apart. Alternatively, dig a shallow furrow along the length of the planting row, lay fertilizer along the bottom, cover with a little soil and then plant seed. Fill in the furrow with light compost or seed raising mix and water in. Seedlings take 1–2 weeks to appear. Thin to 2 in apart (3 in for winter radish) at second leaf stage.
Watering   Water thoroughly to keep soil moist during growing stage.
Fertilizing   Use a complete fertilizer NPK 5:6:4 for furrow planting or dig into garden bed at rate of 4 oz per square yard. Make sure to feed with a recommended liquid fertilizer every week at the seedling stage.
Problems   Caterpillars of the cabbage moth and white butterfly are the main pests to watch out for. Early spraying with appropriate insecticide is recommended. Club root can affect winter radish as this type of radish is left in ground longer than other varieties. Aphids and other insects can be controlled by using pyrethrum or other approved sprays. Make sure that you discontinue using spray a week before harvesting.

HARVESTING

Picking   Pull whole plant from ground at 4–5 weeks. It is a good idea to undertake test pullings to judge size and firmness of fruit when anticipated maturity time is reached. Harvest before radish gets old and tough.

RUTABAGA

Brassica napus var. *napobrassica*

MULTIPLE LEAF SCARS *like those at the tops of these subtly colored rutaba make it easy to distinguish a rutabaga from a turnip.*

FEATURES

Rutabaga is very similar to turnip. It can be identified by the multiple leaf scars which can be seen on its top and the deeply lobed structure of its grayish-green leaves. The large root, which is actually a swelling at the base of the plant's stem, sits on the soil surface as the vegetable grows. The skin is white, yellow or purple and the flesh is creamy to yellow.

CONDITIONS

Climate   Best grown as a cool climate crop, but all climates are suitable, depending on the variety grown.

Aspect   Prefers full sun to partial shade in well-drained soils.

Cultivation   Prepare beds with plenty of organic matter to assist free growth of roots. Beds that have been well fertilized and worked over for a previous crop are ideal as long as earlier crops did not belong to the *Brassica* group. This group includes vegetables such as cabbage, Brussels sprouts and broccoli. Be careful not to let the soil dry out as rutabaga will not do well in dry conditions. Keep beds weed free, being particularly careful not to damage the developing root. Do not hill soil around exposed vegetable.

GROWING METHOD

Planting   For best results plant at end of summer to mid-autumn in hot subtropical areas; late summer to early autumn in temperate zones; and in cold regions have two plantings, one midsummer and the other at the end of winter. Successive planting every 3 weeks ensures a longer harvesting period. Seeds are sown directly into the ground no more than ¼ in deep in rows 10 in apart. Make shallow furrows or seed drill holes along the rows, drop the seeds in, cover with compost and water in. Thin plants to 5 in apart after seedlings appear, which should be within first two weeks after seeds have been sown.

Watering   Needs plenty of water, especially through hot weather periods to avoid plant drying out.

Fertilizing   Prepare bed with a light dressing of poultry manure plus a complete fertilizer NPK 5:7:4 at rate of 2 oz per square yard. Apply side dressings of the same fertilizer about 4 weeks after planting.

Problems   No serious diseases but suffers from various pest infestations. Aphids may be hosed off or controlled with appropriate sprays. Other pests, including caterpillars and grubs, which affect other *Brassica* can also do damage to rutabagas and turnips. Spray with a recommended insecticide every 2 weeks from seedling stage to control pests.

HARVESTING

Picking   Reaches maturity in around 3–4 months, or earlier in warmer areas. The root is not the only part that can be used as the leafy tops of very young plants can be used in salads. When harvesting, pull roots from ground before they become coarse and woody to avoid their developing a very strong flavor.

SHALLOT

Allium ascalonicum, A. cepa

THE CLUSTERED BULBS *at the base of the golden shallot show its kinship with garlic. Shallots are easy to grow and will store well.*

FEATURES

This vegetable is not to be confused with the evergreen onions, known as eschalots or scallions, which are sold in bunches and sometimes called shallots. Scallions are actually very young green onions whereas the shallot is a more mature form of onion, similar to garlic in its form. *A. ascalonicum* is called the golden shallot and has chestnut-brown skin. It has small bulbs, resembling a garlic clove in shape, which measure ¼–1 in in diameter when mature. It has a similar but much more delicate flavor than onion. Elongated varieties have a stronger flavor than the rounder varieties, but are still more subtle in flavor than onions. Belonging to the *Aggregatum* group, the bulbs cluster at the base of the plant with narrow whitish stems and green leaves extending above ground. Used often in French cooking for its subtle flavor. This is an easy vegetable for the home vegetable gardener to grow.

CONDITIONS

Climate Will grow in all climates.
Aspect Prefers full sun to partial shade.
Cultivation Dig in large quantities of animal manure and compost several weeks before planting. Shallow, fibrous roots require light cultivation and beds need to be kept free of weeds.

GROWING METHOD

Planting As this plant does not produce viable seeds it is propagated by replanting small bulbs broken off from the parent plant each season. This happens at the end of summer to beginning of winter in warm tropical areas; from end of summer to end of autumn in temperate zones; from midsummer to mid-autumn in cold regions. If planning to harvest in green state while plant is quite young, plant the bulb quite deep to 2 in and hill soil around the stem as it grows. If planning for mature bulbs, plant quite shallow so that the bulblet is level with the top of the soil. In both cases, it is best to have about 6–8 in space all round each plant.

Watering Water regularly so that soil does not dry out.

Fertilizing Apply complete fertilizer NPK 5:6:4 at rate of 3½ oz per square yard.

Problems Very few pests and diseases. If onion thrips show up, remove them by thorough and vigorous hosing.

HARVESTING

Picking Bulbs mature in 3–4 months, but can be harvested after 8 weeks if soft bulbs with white stalks and young green leaves are preferred. Young succulent leaves may be used in salads or as a flavoring in the same way that chives or scallions are used. Shallots may also be picked at any stage of growth, but care must be taken not to cut the main stem and hinder further development of the plant. Mature bulbs are lifted when top leafy parts wither.

SPINACH

Spinacea oleracea

THE TENDER LEAVES *of spinach spring from a very small root system. There is also a crinkly-leaved variety. Swiss chard, although sometimes called spinach, is a different species.*

SPINACH *NEEDS cool, damp weather and will go to seed in the heat.*

FEATURES

Mature plants of spinach produce a rosette of dark green leaves 4–6 in long with a prominent midrib. The leaves are either crinkled or smooth, depending on variety. Leaves are the edible part of the vegetable and grow in clusters at ground level.

CONDITIONS

Climate   Best in cool climate but crop grows in most areas. Ideal temperatures are 50–60°F.

Aspect   Prefers sun to partial shade in well-drained rich soils and needs shelter from winds.

Cultivation   Prefers non-acidic soils pH range 6.0–7.0, enriched with decayed animal or poultry manure. Lime or dolomite 6 oz per square yard will help neutralize acids. Dig in about 4 lbs of this organic material per square yard two weeks before planting. Keep weeds down by heavy mulching. Mulching will also keep the roots cool.

GROWING METHOD

Planting   Best months to sow are summer through autumn in subtropical climates; late summer through autumn in temperate zones; and autumn through winter in cold areas. Successive sowings every 3 weeks will ensure a continuous crop. Sow seeds directly into the garden bed, ¼ in deep and 12 in apart in rows 14 in apart. Lightly cover seeds with compost and water in so that soil is just moist. Seedlings emerge within 2–3 weeks.

Watering   Soil should be moist, but avoid continual wetting of leaves.

Fertilizing   A week before planting, dig in a complete fertilizer NPK 5:6:4 at rate of 3½ oz per square yard. Regular side feedings of a nitrogen-rich fertilizer after the first appearance of seedlings will promote good leaf growth.

Problems   Spinach blight will cause leaves to yellow and then curl up and die as a result of infection by the cucumber mosaic virus. Downy mildew causes pale patches on leaves. Leaf miners and mites are main pests. All these should be controlled by an appropriate fungicide or insect sprays.

HARVESTING

Picking   Crops take 8–10 weeks to mature. Pick individual leaves as required or pull the whole plant from the ground.

SQUASH
Cucurbita

DELICATE-SKINNED *green and yellow squash showing the typical scalloped edging. They make an attractive addition to the dinner plate.*

FEATURES

Summer squash is considered under this heading. A number of summer and winter squash are now available, all being warm weather crops. Like marrows and squash, summer squash have soft skins and are picked and eaten when immature, although there are some oddities within the family. Gramma or trombone (*C. moschata*) is a mature form of summer squash used for pies or tarts. The growing habit of the mature plant is similar to a bush rather than a vine. It is like a cucurbita in all other respects.

CONDITIONS

Climate   A warm weather crop, sensitive to cold and frosts. Can be grown in most areas but the colder it gets the shorter the season.

Aspect   Prefers full sun to partial shade in a wide range of soils. Good drainage is essential.

Cultivation   Heavy feeders, preferring well-fertilized soil. Dig in plenty of well-rotted manure and compost several weeks ahead of planting. Keep free of weeds and other decaying matter which might harbor disease. Shallow cultivate, trying not to disturb delicate root structure. If no fruit develops it may be due to unsuitable weather or lack of bee activity. which may occur when small varieties grow indoors. If this happens hand-pollination of male and female flowers may be necessary.

GROWING METHOD

Planting   Plant seeds all year round in hot, subtropical climates; in spring in temperate zones; only in early summer in cold regions. Raise seeds in pots 4–5 weeks ahead of planting out in the open garden. Plant seeds ⅘ in deep in seed-raising mix. Alternatively, sow direct into garden soil in final growing position. Place several seeds ½ in deep in wide, hollow saucer-shaped depressions. Depressions should be 8 in deep, the excavated soil being built or hilled up as a rim around edge of the depression. Leave 3 ft of garden space between "hills." Thin to two or three plants at seedling stage and to one healthy plant when true leaves appear. Be careful not to disturb root structure, removing seedlings by cutting stems at ground level. If planting in rows, have a clear 5–6 ft space around each plant.

Watering   Keep water up to plant but off the stems and foliage, especially when fruit is setting. Moisture retentiveness of soil will depend on structure with sandy soil needing more watering than heavier soil. Lack of water may cause partly formed fruit to fall. Large leaf structure wilts in hot weather but recovers if soil is moist.

Fertilizing   Dig in 3½ oz complete fertilizer NPK 5:6:6 just before sowing. Side dressings of ¾ oz urea per square yard when first fruit has set can be applied and watered in immediately. Too much fertilizer will promote vigorous green growth at the expense of fruit development.

Problems   Powdery mildew and bacterial wilt are common. Prevention is important. Do not handle fragile vines while wet and keep garden clean. Insects spread diseases such as viral mosaic. Infected plants should be sprayed on upper and lower leaves or removed altogether. Aphids and pumpkin beetle affecting early growth, especially in spring, should be sprayed.

HARVESTING

Picking   Squash mature in 12–14 weeks, but are often harvested earlier before skin hardens.

SWEET CORN

Zea mays var. saccharata

SHORT ROWS *of sweet corn are placed back-to-back in a well-planned garden. Corn needs plenty of space, but it's easy to grow and tastes much sweeter than the supermarket version.*

THE DELICATE SILK *of the maturing corn cob will darken as the kernels ripen.*

FEATURES

A member of the grass family growing to 15 ft tall, producing 1–2 ears per stalk. These ears or cobs are completely covered with regularly arranged seeds called kernels which are white to yellow, although some varieties have red and black seeds or a combination of all these colors.

CONDITIONS

Climate Prefers hot or warm, frost-free climates.
Aspect Needs full sun and wind breaks, if necessary.
Cultivation Beds should be heavily fertilized and watered during growing cycle. Remove weeds by light cultivation. Corn is pollinated by the fall of pollen from male flowers (tassels) at the top of the stem onto female flowers (silks) lower down. When watering at this stage, keep spray at ground level and not over tassels or silks.

GROWING METHOD

Planting Plant all year in tropical and subtropical climates (autumn is best time); in spring to midsummer in temperate zones; and late spring to early summer in cold regions. Dig in poultry manure at least two weeks before planting. Prepare short rather than long rows 20–24 in apart to give a clumping effect to bed. Dig seed trenches in rows to a depth of 10 in, layer with complete fertilizer, then cover with 4 in soil. Space seeds 10 in apart. Needs damp and warm soil, at least 60°F. Seedlings will emerge within 14 days.

Watering Keep soil moist, especially in hot weather and after pollination when care should be taken not to wet tassels.

Fertilizing Give applications of fertilizer high in nitrogen and phosphate, NPK 6:6:4 at the planting stage and further side applications throughout the growing stage.

Problems Has many pests including corn earworm, corn borer and cutworm which penetrate ears and damage the seed. Leaf-sucking aphids are also a problem. At the first sign of trouble, spray with appropriate insecticide every 2 or 3 days at green silk stage. Birds may attack the ears. Cover at ripening stage.

HARVESTING

Picking Reaches maturity within 12–14 weeks when kernels are plump and full of milk. Clear fluid means the cob is immature.

SWEET POTATO

Ipomoea batatas

THE SWEET POTATO'S *flesh can be white, cream or orange-colored, but all varieties have a starchy texture and fragile skin.*

FEATURES

This is an ornamental vine with small, white or pink to dark purple flowers. Edible parts are the thick elongated tubers which can have white, creamy-yellow or deep orange flesh. Sweet potatoes are classified as being moist or dry, depending on their cooking texture. Those with moist flesh are sometimes called yams. This frost-tender, warm season perennial (grown as an annual) is not suitable for container growing. This sweet-tasting vegetable may be cooked in a variety of ways and is an excellent vegetable to have in the home garden.

CONDITIONS

Climate Needs warm days and nights and to be free of frosts for at least 4–6 months during the growing season. Sweet potato is hard to grow in cool to cold climates.

Aspect Prefers to be grown in full sun. It does not like cool soil.

Cultivation Grows best in sandy or sandy loam soils. It is important to control weed growth before vines start rapid growth. The dense vine will prevent most weed growth once it develops. Sweet potatoes have a deep root system so garden beds may need to be raised, especially when grown in areas where there are heavy clay soils.

GROWING METHOD

Planting Plant all year round in tropical zones; and from spring to midsummer in subtropical and warm coastal regions. Sweet potatoes are grown from rooted sprouts or shoots called slips which are taken from mature healthy tubers. Tubers are placed in propagating beds and covered with 3 in of sand or light soil. The bed should be kept moist and warm. When shoots appear and have grown to 6 in, they are gently pulled out and transplanted. Tubers usually then go on to produce a second lot of slips for transplanting. Plant slips, not too deeply, in open garden beds 14 in apart and with 3 ft between rows. The rows should be ridged or hilled to a height of 10 in for best results. Water the plants immediately.

Watering Water well at the initial planting stage and maintain even soil moisture levels throughout the growing period. If the soil is too wet or waterlogged, tuber rot may set in. Do not water during the month before harvesting.

Fertilizing Before planting dig in 3 1/2 oz complete fertilizer, NPK 5:6:4 per square yard, and perhaps give a side dressing of urea 2 months after planting. Do not fertilize with poultry manure or nitrogen rich fertilizers as this only promotes leaf growth instead of tuber development.

Problems There are generally no problems but it is advisable to rotate sweet potato crops every 2–3 years. Maintaining general garden health is the best preventative measure you can adopt.

HARVESTING

Picking It takes around 5–6 months for the sweet potato vine to reach maturity, white-fleshed tubers taking longer than earlier maturing orange-fleshed varieties. Harvest the tubers before any cold snaps set in and be very careful not to damage the thin skins when lifting them from ground.

SWISS CHARD

Beta vulgaris var. *cicla*

THE LARGE, CRINKLY LEAVES *of Swiss chard can feature white, orange, gold or sometimes red stems. It is very easy to grow.*

FEATURES

Swiss chard is a member of the beet family and is often mistakenly called spinach. Swiss chard has white to cream ribbed stems with large, green, crinkly leaves. All these parts are edible. Varieties of chard are available with varicolored (bright red, orange, gold and yellow) stems. These are the rainbow chards. Swiss chard is easy to grow in the home vegetable garden.

CONDITIONS

Climate   All climate zones are suitable. Best to avoid growing in very hot or frosty cold months.

Aspect   Prefers full sun or partial shade with good soil drainage.

Cultivation   Grows very quickly and should mature within 8–12 weeks of planting. It may bolt to seed in hot weather. Remove the flower stems as they appear. Keep beds free of weeds and mulch in hot weather. It is important to maintain feeding during the growing period.

GROWING METHOD

Planting   Plant all year round in subtropical climates, midwinter to early summer in temperate zones, and late summer and during spring in colder areas. The main rule is not to sow in winter months. Sowing seeds direct into the garden or transplanting seedlings are acceptable methods of planting. Prepare beds with plenty of compost or decayed manure, at least 2 lbs per square yard, and see that soils are alkaline. To sow seeds direct, dig shallow trenches along garden rows which should be 16 in apart. Apply fertilizer along each side of the trench base, fill with soil and firm down. Open up trenches with seed drills to a depth of 3/4–1 in. Cover seeds and water in. Seedlings should appear within 2 weeks. When 1 in high, thin to 12 in apart.

Watering   Keep soil moist by regular waterings.

Fertilizing   Swiss chard likes nitrogen-rich fertilizers. Use a complete fertilizer NPK 6:6:6 at a rate of 3 1/2 oz per square yard. Apply monthly side dressings of 3/4 oz urea per square yard to achieve a vigorous growth.

Problems   Leaf spot, a disease affecting spring plantings whereby gray surface spots and brown edges appear on the leaves, should be treated with appropriate sprays or else the infected leaves should be picked and burned. Aphids and leaf miners can be controlled by vigorous hosing or by picking insects off the plant.

HARVESTING

Picking   Swiss chard will have a long harvest period if seed is sown at the right time (see Planting). The mature outside leaves are picked as the need arises and usually when they are 4–8 in long. Do not cut the stalks but break or peel off by a downwards and sideways action. Leave younger stalks on the parent plant to encourage further growth. Alternatively, the whole plant can be harvested by cutting down to 2 in and then left to regenerate.

TARO ROOT

Alocasia macrorrhiza, syn. *Colocasia esculenta*

A TARO TUBER *in cross-section reveals the starchy flesh which lies beneath its thick, fibrous skin. The leaves of the plant are also edible.*

FEATURES

Also known under the common name of dasheen, this is an edible tuber with a high starch level similar to that of the potato, but with a lower water content. The flesh ranges through white to purplish or greenish. The tuber has a spherical shape, growing to 8 in with a thick, fibrous, hairy light brown skin, and is characterized by divisional markings on the circumference. It is a large plant growing to 3–4 ft with large, light green, shield-shaped leaves resembling elephants' ears which are borne on long stalks. The leaves, sometimes called "callaloo," are also edible and sometimes grown purely for their decorative quality. This vegetable is eaten in many tropical countries throughout the world, and is particularly popular in the West Indies.

CONDITIONS

Climate	Requires warm climates with long hot summers. Does best in tropical and subtropical areas with temperatures around 95°F.
Aspect	Taro prefers full sun with warm, moist well-drained soils.
Cultivation	The tubers cannot be cultivated in frost-prone areas. Keep soil fertile and moist. Sometimes the plant is "forced" in warm dark conditions to produce blanched leaves which are considered a delicacy by food lovers.

GROWING METHOD

Planting	Plant autumn and winter in warm zones and in midsummer to mid-winter in tropical areas. Small tubers, called "sons of taro" and taken from the parent tuber, are planted during spring. These are planted in furrows or trenches 6 in deep and spaced 14 in apart in rows about 3 ft apart. After planting, cover tubers with 2 in soil and water in. They are best grown near some other irrigation ditch with its associated water run-off. Propagation may also be by stem cuttings.
Watering	Needs a great deal of regular watering during growth cycle.
Fertilizing	Rich, fertile, friable soil containing plenty of organic material to which a complete fertilizer NPK 5:6:4 has been added is best. Do not overfertilize with nitrogen as this will promote excessive leaf growth at the expense of the tuber.
Problems	Relatively free of any specific pests or diseases.

HARVESTING

Picking	Taro matures in 3–7 months, depending on variety. At maturity, the leaves turn yellow and the plant almost dies. When this happens carefully lift the tubers from the soil, especially if there is any danger of a cold spell as this will cause damage to the tuber. Young leaves and stems are also edible and should be picked as soon as the leaves open. However, never strip plant fully as some leaves are necessary for the continuing successful development of the tuber.

TOMATO

Lycopersicon esculentum

SOFT-STEMMED *tomato plants need to be staked to prevent wind damage and to give support to the developing fruit.*

BE VIGILANT *when cultivating tomatoes: maturing plants need constant protection from marauding pests and diseases.*

FEATURES

Tomato has a weak, soft-stemmed structure with alternate lobed and toothed leaves. Mature plant has a vine-like or bush-growing habit. Yellow flowers grow in clusters and produce fruit of varying sizes which may be red, yellow, or orange to creamy white, depending on variety. Tomatoes are a heavy-yielding crop and a favorite of home gardeners. They are also excellent for container growing, some small fruiting varieties even suited to growing in hanging baskets.

CONDITIONS

Climate   Varieties of tomato have been developed which are suitable to all climatic conditions. However, basically this is a warm season vegetable (technically a fruit), susceptible to frosts.

Aspect   Prefers full sun to partial shade. Although preferring full sun, tomato may be affected by sunscald in very hot climates. These plants require good drainage and protection from strong winds.

Cultivation   Prepare beds with animal manure, 4 lbs per square yard about a month before planting. Dig in to spade depth. A little fertilizer may be placed under seedlings, with no additions until first fruit has set. Overfertilizing with nitrogen leads to excessive leaf growth. Weak stems need securing against wind damage and to give support for heavy fruit. Use 6 ft stakes and fix firmly in soil at planting to prevent root damage in growing plant. As plant grows, secure to stake with soft ties at 12 in intervals. Prune by picking out lateral shoots at junctions of leaf stalks and main stem. Single lateral shoots can be left to elongate and form another stem.

GROWING METHOD

Planting   Sow seeds all year in warm tropical climates; late autumn to early summer in temperate zones; during spring in cold regions. Seeds may be planted 1/5 in deep, directly into the garden, but are usually germinated in seed trays. Seedlings will appear in about 14 days. When 4 in tall they may be picked out into smaller containers and hardened for two weeks. Transplant when about 8–10 in tall, planted 24 in apart in rows 24 in apart.

TOMATO VARIETIES

Cherry: Juicy with thin skin and a sweet, strong flavor. Good in salads

Vine ripened: Full, intense flavor when picked at this stage. Any variety may be ripened on the vine

Yellow pear: Delicate skin and bland flavor. Decorative in salads

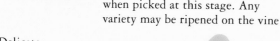

Common: Firm and full flavored when harvested from the home vegetable garden

Roma or egg: Firm flesh, few seeds and full flavor. Excellent for sauces, canning and sun-drying

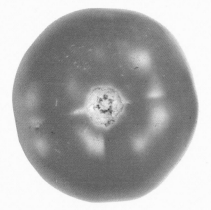

Watering	Plenty of water is needed during growth cycle so do not let soil dry out. Uneven watering leads to blossom-end rot. Do not water over the plants by sprinkler method. Irrigate along furrows between the rows.
Fertilizing	Phosphorus, an important nutrient, must be provided, especially at seedling stage. Lack of it leads to low yields. Dig in complete fertilizer NPK 8:11:10 at a rate of 3 oz per square yard before planting, or fertilize under seedlings.

Problems	Prone to spotted wilt spread by thrips. Immature fruit becomes blotched or mottled and stunted foliage turns purplish. Leaf or target spot is common in wet seasons but also caused by excessive use of nitrogen. Mites, tomato caterpillar and fruit fly are other pests. All can be controlled by appropriate sprays. Rotate crops if soil disease is endemic.

HARVESTING

Picking	Crop matures in 3–5 months, depending on variety. Fruit is picked when ripe on bush, or at mature green stage and ripened indoors.

TURNIP

Brassica rapa

ALTHOUGH THE LEAVES *of the turnip can be eaten, it is mainly grown for its root. The reddish tip develops when it is mature.*

FEATURES

A vegetable closely associated with the rutabaga. The large root, which is actually a swelling at the base of the stem, sits on the soil surface as the vegetable grows. The turnip comes in a variety of shapes and sizes. It has white flesh and skin supporting a rosette of green feathery leaves. Both leaves and root are edible, although turnip is mainly grown for the root which is often used in soups and stews. The leafy tops of young vegetables can be used in salads.

CONDITIONS

Climate   Best grown as a cool climate crop but all climates suit, depending on variety of turnip grown.

Aspect   Prefers full sun to partial shade and well-drained soils.

Cultivation   Garden beds should be well prepared with plenty of organic matter before planting to assist free growth of roots. Those beds that have been well fertilized and worked over for a previous crop are ideal as long as the earlier crop did not belong to the *Brassica* group, which includes vegetables such as cabbages, Brussels sprouts or broccoli. Keep beds watered and do not let soil dry out. Keep free of weeds, removing by hand if necessary so that the developing root is not damaged. Do not hill soil around the exposed vegetable.

GROWING METHOD

Planting   Best times to plant are late summer to early autumn in hot subtropical areas; midsummer to mid-autumn in temperate zones; with two plantings in cold regions, one in late summer and the other in winter to early spring. Successive planting every 3 weeks ensures a longer harvest. Sow seeds into ground no more than 1/4 in deep in rows 10 in apart. Make shallow furrows or seed drill holes along the rows, drop the seeds in, cover with compost and water in. Thin plants to 4 in apart after seedlings appear which should be within the first two weeks after seeds are sown.

Watering   Require plenty of water, especially through any periods of particularly hot weather.

Fertilizing   Prepare bed with a light dressing of poultry manure plus a complete fertilizer NPK 5:7:4 at rate of 2 oz per square yard. Apply side dressings of the same fertilizer about four weeks after planting.

Problems   Turnips have no serious diseases but do suffer from pest infestations. Aphids may be hosed off or controlled with appropriate sprays. Caterpillars and grubs that affect other *Brassica* can also do damage to turnips. Spraying with a recommended insecticide every 2 weeks from seedling stage onwards will help to alleviate these problems in the home garden.

HARVESTING

Picking   Reaches maturity in 2–3 months, or earlier in warmer areas. Pull whole roots from the ground before they become coarse and woody and develop an over-strong flavor. If the seeds have been sown thickly there will be an abundance of seedlings. In this case harvest within 8 weeks of planting as both root and leaf are good to eat at this stage.

WATER CHESTNUT

Eleocharis dulcis

THE WATER CHESTNUT'S *brown corms are sustained by reed-like leaves which protrude from the water and supply air to the roots.*

FEATURES

This is a root vegetable which does not belong to the chestnut family at all. A perennial reed-like plant, the slender cylindrical and thinly hollow leaves, 3–6 ft in length, act as air pumps taking oxygen to the roots as well as helping to purify the water in which the plant grows. The edible corm, about the size of a walnut and 2 in across, grows underwater at the end of horizontal rhizomes (underground stems). The corm changes from pale to dark mahogany-brown as it matures. The whitish flesh has a sweet nutty flavor which is similar to the flavor of coconut or macadamia. Corms are first peeled and can then be eaten raw or cooked. They have a firm crisp texture. Water chestnuts are the only nuts that are known as vegetables.

CONDITIONS

Climate   Best grown in climates with hot summers, with temperatures above 86°F during leafy stage of growth and above 68°F when corms are forming.

Aspect   Grows in shallow water containers or ponds and usually not affected by weather extremes.

Cultivation   Very little care needed except to see water in container or pond does not dry out. Rhizomes spread horizontally under the soil surface, turning up to form suckers and new plants. Later come the food-producing rhizomes or corms.

GROWING METHOD

Planting   Corms are planted in spring after any cool snaps have passed. After summer harvest and during cooler periods before planting, corms should be stored in moist sand or loose damp soil. They can be planted into any shallow, fresh water aquatic environment such as dams, small garden ponds, aquariums or containers that will hold water. Plant corm and heap soil around, holding or fixing in place with small stones. At least 4 in soil is required with a covering of 1 in water. Use only rich, clay or peaty, fertile soils with an ideal pH range of 6.9–7.3. To achieve this pH range, add a couple of handfuls of lime or dolomite to the soil. Water chestnuts, however, will tolerate a variety of conditions, even those of slight salinity.

Watering   Not essential when in aquatic environment.

Fertilizing   No chemical fertilizing is required as long as soil used has been enriched with a lot of well-composted organic matter and old animal manure.

Problems   No diseases are known. Plant is very hardy but as it is grown in water, mosquito larvae may be a problem. Introduce goldfish or tadpoles into the aquatic environment or sprinkle quassia chips over surface of water.

HARVESTING

Picking   Require around a 6-month growing season at the end of which stem tops turn brown and die down. The darkish skin should be tight and taut but if the flesh texture is mushy the nut is too old. Harvest during winter although the vegetable will not deteriorate if left in soil for longer periods.

WHITE RADISH

Raphanus sativus var. *longipinnatus* and var. *radicola*

THE SWOLLEN, ELONGATED *taproot of the white radish is prized by the Japanese. It is eaten cooked, and often pickled.*

FEATURES

This is an oriental form of radish often called the Japanese daikon which means "big root." It is a member of the mustard family and various types are used in Japanese and Chinese cuisines. These cuisines also use other parts of the plant including leaves, stems, seed pods and seedlings in food preparations. The shape of the swollen tap root varies from spherical to elongated and triangular, depending on variety; its flesh is white to greenish. The plant itself has an erect nature, growing to 12–24 in. It will grow to over 3 ft when left to grow to flowering stage. The non-branching stem supports a leafy rosette composed of large, sprawling, lobed leaves which are green to grayish and sometimes splashed with purple.

CONDITIONS

Climate Best grown as a cool weather crop with an ideal growing temperature range around 68°F. The most important thing to remember is to choose the variety most suited to your local climate.

Aspect Prefers moist, shady spots with rich, light and well-drained soils.

Cultivation Keep beds free of weeds and avoid damage to roots at all times as any damage will increase the risk of disease. These plants have a tendency to bolt in warm conditions after cold snaps.

GROWING METHOD

Planting Sow twice a year in spring and autumn in tropical and warm areas, and in autumn in cool regions. Root shape tends to be modified by the character of the soil so heavy clay soils, which prevent roots expanding, should be avoided if possible. Some varieties have been adapted whereby the root tends to prop itself above the soil level. Sow seeds thinly ¼–¾ in deep in holes 1 in deep directly into the garden bed. Seedlings will appear in 10–14 days. Thin so that young plants are at least 4 in apart depending on variety. Really large rooting types will need up to 16 in space all round each plant. As the seedlings grow, their stems can be covered with soil from around the drill holes.

Watering Water steadily and constantly and do not let soil dry out. As plants reach maturity, cut down on watering as excess water leads to cracking of roots.

Fertilizing Preferably use old fertilized beds. If necessary, use complete fertilizer NPK 5:6:4 beneath drill holes before planting.

Problems Aphids, cabbage white butterfly, nematodes and black beetle cause root damage. Control with pyrethrum sprays. Soil diseases such as bacterial soft rot affect root at ground level gradually sending whole root soft and mushy. Bacteria present in decaying vegetable matter in the soil is the main cause and hot, wet weather will favor the disease. Handle vegetable carefully during cultivation and destroy any diseased plants. Rotate crops at least every 3 years as a preventative measure.

HARVESTING

Picking Radish matures within 8–10 weeks in most areas but can be harvested at any stage of the growing cycle. Roots are ready when about 8 in long (elongated varieties) or 2–4 in across. Skins should be smooth and white and flesh firm. Harvest during cool weather, pulling root whole from ground.

WITLOOF

Cichorium intybus

BLANCHING THE LEAVES *of witloof during growth will prevent the development of the bitterness often associated with this vegetable.*

FEATURES

Variously known as Belgian endive or Brussels chicory, witloof is a member of the chicory family, being the blanched, lettuce-like heart of the chicory plant. During growing the head is forced to grow into a compact form with pointed white leaves with green or yellow tips. Has a bittersweet taste, leaf greenness indicating bitterness.

CONDITIONS

Climate   Best grown as a cool season crop.
Aspect   Prefers direct or partial sunlight until put in controlled dark environment for blanching.

Cultivation   Seeds planted in spring may require heavier feeding to produce advanced growth by autumn. At this point, plants are lifted to undergo the second stage of cultivation, that is the forcing and blanching of the plant. Tops of the plants are cut off to within 2 in of root just above the crown. Plants are then placed upright in a box or container, which can be covered to exclude sunlight, and topped with 6 in of loose soil. This prevents bitterness developing in leaves. The container should be kept in a dark place at not less than 50°F.

GROWING METHOD

Planting   Sow seeds during spring through to early summer directly into the garden beds. Plant seeds ¼ in deep and in rows 12 in apart. Seeds can be planted closely together and then thinned to 10 in apart when seedlings appear in approximately 10–14 days. Mulch around young plants to keep weeds down and to keep soil moist. From sowing until lifting (see Cultivation) is known as the first stage of growth. During the second stage the plants are lifted and placed in a dark box or container until they reach maturity.

Watering   Needs regular watering to keep soil moist, especially through hotter summer months of growth. This encourages development and prevents bitterness developing in the leaves.

Fertilizing   Prefers old or previously fertilized beds from another crop. Freshly manured soil is likely to cause forking of the roots. If extra feeding is required, use complete fertilizer NPK 5:6:4, applied at a rate of 3½ oz per square yard of garden bed.

Problems   Unlikely to be affected by pests or diseases.

HARVESTING

Picking   Witloof takes about 4 months to mature from time of planting seed. The second stage of the cultivation or blanching process takes 8–12 weeks by which time the witloof will be 6–8 in long and ready for harvest. Harvest only as necessary as the witloof should be used fairly soon. Once picked it is a good idea to keep stored in the refrigerator as it will become bitter if exposed to light. A second crop can be encouraged if witloof is broken off, rather than being cut, when picked. Witloof is surprisingly easy for the home gardener to cultivate.

ZUCCHINI

Cucurbita pepo

THE ZUCCHINI FRUIT DEVELOPS *from the base of the yellow flower. This attractive plant will also do well in containers.*

FEATURES

Zucchini are actually related to marrow squash and picked when they are quite young. They are also known as courgettes in Europe. Zucchini grow on bushes and are quite prolific and are ideal specimens for containers. The vegetable is elongated in shape (although tear-shaped varieties exist) and dark green through to yellow, reaching 6–8 in at maturity. Young zucchini may be sliced and eaten raw in salads, and older zucchini are excellent for cooking.

CONDITIONS

Climate A warm weather crop, sensitive to cold and frosts. Grows in most areas but the colder it gets the shorter the growing season. Does well indoors and in locations where conditions can be controlled to suit the growing plant.

Aspect Prefers full sun to partial shade and a wide range of soils with good drainage.

Cultivation Zucchini are heavy feeders and like heavily fertilized soil so dig in plenty of well-rotted manure and compost several weeks ahead of planting. Keep areas around bush free of weeds and other decaying matter which might harbor disease. Cultivate lightly, trying not to disturb root structure. If no fruit develops it may be due to unsuitable weather or lack of bee activity around flowers. In this case, hand-pollination of male and female flowers will be necessary if the bush is to bear fruit.

GROWING METHOD

Planting Plant all year round in hot, subtropical climates, in spring in temperate zones, and in early summer in cold regions. Raise seeds in pots 4–5 weeks ahead of planting out in open garden. Plant seeds ⅘ in deep in seed-raising mix or sow direct in final growing position. Place several seeds ½ in deep in wide, hollow saucer-shaped depressions. Depressions should be 8 in deep, the excavated soil being built or hilled up as a rim at the edge. Leave 3 ft of garden space between "hills." Thin to two or three plants at seedling stage and finally to one healthy plant when true leaves appear. Remove seedlings by cutting stems at ground level taking care not to disturb root structure. If planting in rows, leave about 3 ft of space between plants.

Watering Keep water up to plant but off stems and foliage, especially when fruit is setting. Moisture retentiveness of soil depends on structure, with sandy soils needing more water than heavier ones. Lack of water may cause partly formed fruit to fall. Leaves wilt during hot weather but recover if soil is kept moist.

Fertilizing Dig in 3½ oz complete fertilizer NPK 5:6:6 just before sowing. Side dressings of ¾ oz urea per square yard watered in immediately when first fruit has set can be applied. However, remember too much fertilizer will promote vigorous green growth at the expense of development of fruit.

Problems Powdery mildew and bacterial wilt are common. Preventative care is important. Do not handle fragile vines while wet and keep garden clean. Diseases include viral mosaic. Infected plants should be sprayed on upper and lower leaves or removed from garden. Aphids and pumpkin beetle affecting early growth, especially in spring, should be controlled by spraying.

HARVESTING

Picking Harvest when 4–6 in long and skin is soft. Constant picking will prolong flowering.

NAME	STORAGE
ARTICHOKE, GLOBE	Harvested buds will keep in a cool place for several weeks or in the refrigerator for no more than two weeks. Keep them dry in an airtight crisper or plastic bag.
ASPARAGUS	Fresh asparagus will keep in the refrigerator for 7–10 days after being harvested. Break off the rough ends and stand upright in 1 in water.
BEAN, BROAD	Freshly harvested pods will keep in refrigerator for up to two weeks. Shelled beans can be dried, or preserved by canning.
BEAN, FRENCH, CLIMBING, DWARF	Do not wash the vegetable after harvest. Freshly picked beans will keep in refrigerator for up to a week or they can be successfully canned or pickled when mature.
BEET	Swollen roots of the beet will keep for up to 3 weeks in the refrigerator and the leaves for up to a week if stored in an airtight plastic bag. Roots can be pickled or canned.
BROCCOLI	Heads will keep in refrigerator for up to a week, after which vegetable gradually turns yellow and becomes tasteless.
BRUSSELS SPROUT	Early winter sprouts left on the stem and hung in a cool dry place will keep for up to a month. Singly harvested, they will keep for 7–10 days in the refrigerator. In both cases, first remove all the loose and discolored leaves from the plant and only wash the vegetables just before you are ready to use them in cooking.
CABBAGE	These will keep for several weeks in the crisper compartment of the refrigerator. Pickled as sauerkraut, cabbage makes a delicious preserve.
CARROT	Like potatoes, carrots can be stored in the ground in cool winter areas. The soils must be kept well drained and not water logged. Leave the leafy tops attached. Once harvested, the top can be removed and the carrots stored in containers packed with dry sand. Keep stored in a cool position. Carrots will also keep crisp in refrigerator for 4 weeks or so if protected in plastic bags. They are delicious if pickled or canned.
CAULIFLOWER	Heads will keep up to a week in the refrigerator. Florets can also be pickled.
CELERY	Celery stalks will keep crisp for up to 10 days in refrigerator. Leaves can be dried and chopped and used as a dried herb for flavoring purposes. Seeds are also dried and used in soups and pickles.
CHAYOTE	Freshly picked chayote will keep in vegetable crisper of refrigerator for 1–2 weeks.
CHILIES	Keep in a cool, dark place for up to a week or in a sealed container in refrigerator for 3 weeks. Chilies are also excellent when dried.

VEGETABLES

NAME	STORAGE
CHINESE BROCCOLI	Keeps in crisper compartment of refrigerator for up to a week.
CHINESE CABBAGE	Keeps fresh in refrigerator for several weeks, even months, in cool, dry places such as a cellar. When ready to use, discard outer discolored and battered leaves to reveal firm, central head. Never store in plastic bags.
CHINESE SPINACH	Leaves go limp soon after harvesting. Young shoot pickings are best eaten immediately and are good in salads. Older leaves can be stored in refrigerator crisper but will not keep for more than a few days. Steam or cook in same way that you would cook other leafy vegetables.
CUCUMBER	Will keep in refrigerator for 7–10 days but at very cold temperatures the flesh will turn soft and translucent, rendering the cucumber inedible. It is ideal for pickling, especially if fruit is picked when young, that is at the "gherkin" stage and 2–3 in in length.
EGGPLANT	Recently cropped fruit will keep for 7–10 days in a cool spot. It is ideal for pickling.
ENDIVE	Will keep for up to two weeks in crisper compartment of refrigerator, the inner leaves being best for salads.
FENNEL	Fennel leaves do not keep for more than a couple of days in the refrigerator.
GARLIC	Leaves are left attached to bulb then left to dry in clumps in full sun for a few days. On no account let bulbs get wet. Move inside if rain threatens. Hang in an open mesh bag in a dry, airy position.
GINGER	Mature rhizomes store well in cool dry places. If stored in the natural state for too long however, the flesh will become dry and the flavor turns towards bitterness. Dried ginger can be ground into powder.
JERUSALEM ARTICHOKE	As with other root crops, the simplest method of storing is to leave the tuber in the ground, digging up only when necessary and thus having a ready supply out of season. Harvested vegetables will keep for a month in dark cool places away from intense cold. Pack into boxes and surround tubers with peat moss.
KOHLRABI	Bulbs can be stored in refrigerator for 7–10 days.
LEEK	Will keep 7–10 days in refrigerator.
LETTUCE	Will keep 7–10 days in crisper section of refrigerator.
MARROW SQUASH	Handle carefully and do not wash or brush skin of fruit before usage to prevent skin damage. Squash will keep for up to a week in refrigerator.

NAME		STORAGE
MUSHROOM		Mushrooms can be stored in the refrigerator (not in plastic bags or they will sweat) for around 5–7 days. They can also be dried or pickled and stored in bottles.
OKRA		Pods may be used fresh or dried. They are widely used as a flavoring in soups and in meat cooking, or can be fried or boiled and eaten as a vegetable.
ONION		Store bulbs in a cool, dry place in an open-weave mesh basket to allow free air circulation around them. Do not store close to other vegetables.
PARSNIP		Parsnips can be kept in ground 2–3 months after reaching maturity in cool–cold climates, but see that beds are kept reasonably dry during this storage period. Low temperatures convert starches to sugars giving a sweet root. Freshly harvested vegetables will keep in refrigerator 2–3 weeks, slightly less in cool dry cupboards where they tend to lose their firmness.
PEA		Pods keep for a short time in the refrigerator. The seeds will lose a great deal of their sugar content within a few days, converting it to starch.
PEPPER		Sweet peppers will keep for up to a week in the refrigerator. They can also be grilled or baked, and with the skins and seeds removed, preserved in spicy vinegars. Hot peppers can be dried successfully.
POTATO		Keep harvest in a cool, dark airy place and exclude sunlight to prevent skin becoming tinged with green. Young or "new" potatoes will not store for long periods.
PUMPKIN		Handle carefully and do not wash or brush skin of fruit before storing. It will keep for several months in a cool, airy place or in boxes. Check occasionally for rotting or damage to skin and flesh by vermin.
RADISH		Radish will keep for a week to 10 days in the crisper section of the refrigerator.
RUTABAGA		Rutabagas have a long storage time and can be kept in or out of the refrigerator.
SHALLOT		Bulbs will keep in a cold, dry place for several months or the flesh may be chopped and frozen similarly to onions.
SNOW PEA		Pods keep for a short time in the refrigerator but will lose a great deal of their sugar content within a few days, converting it to starch.
SPINACH		Spinach leaves will keep in refrigerator for up to a week but they are better if eaten immediately.

VEGETABLES

NAME		STORAGE
SQUASH		Handle carefully and do not wash or brush skin of fruit before usage to prevent skin damage. They will keep for up to a week in refrigerator.
SUGAR SNAP PEA		Pods keep for a short time in the refrigerator. The seeds will lose a great deal of their sugar content within a few days, converting it to starch.
SWEET CORN		Sweet corn means there is plenty of sugar in the vegetable when it is harvested. The sugar soon turns to starch and the vegetable loses a great deal of its flavor, so freshly picked corn should be eaten as soon as possible. Storing in the refrigerator for a couple of days will slow down the sugar loss. Alternatively, kernels can be stripped from the cob and then frozen.
SWEET POTATO		Very easy vegetable to store but do not wash before putting away. Will keep for at least 4 months in this condition. Do not store in refrigerated conditions below 50°F.
SWISS CHARD		Swiss chard will keep for up to 2 weeks in crisper part of refrigerator but is best eaten when freshly picked before leaves become limp.
TARO ROOT		Will keep for several months in cool, dry storage spots. Taro must always be cooked before eating. Young leaves are boiled twice, discarding water in between, then pureed and eaten or frozen for later consumption.
TOMATO		Tomatoes will keep between 2–4 weeks in refrigerator although they tend to lose their flavor over long periods. They can be pulped then bottled or processed into soups and sauces and frozen.
TURNIP		Turnips do not store as long as rutabagas but, like them, can be kept in or out of the refrigerator.
WATER CHESTNUT		Examine the vegetable for rotten spots and remove damaged corms. The unpeeled harvest will keep in bags in the refrigerator for up to 2 weeks. If peeled in advance of use store in cold water in refrigerator to prevent browning, again for up to 2 weeks, but water must be changed daily. Chestnuts can be dried and ground to a flour. Commercial crops are cooked and preserved by canning, flavor and texture being lost in the process.
WHITE RADISH		If root has developed a hollowness inside, it will not store long, but generally will keep in refrigerator at very low temperatures for several weeks. They can be eaten raw, cooked, dried, pickled, fermented or preserved in brine.
WITLOOF		Witloof does not store well and becomes limp soon after exposure to light. May be kept in refrigerator for a few days but a greening of leaves from exposure to light indicates developing bitter taste.
ZUCCHINI		Handle carefully and do not wash or brush skin of fruit before usage. They will keep for up to a week in refrigerator.

NAME	TO FREEZE
ARTICHOKE, GLOBE	Remove outer leaves. Wash, trim stalks and remove "chokes" and blanch them, a few at a time, for 7 minutes. Cool in iced water for 7 minutes, drain. Pack in freezer bags, remove air from bags, seal and label. Freeze for up to 6 months.
ASPARAGUS	Wash and remove woody portions and scales of spears, cut into 6 in lengths and blanch in boiling water for 3 minutes. Cool in iced water for 3 minutes, drain. Place on trays in a single layer and freeze for 30 minutes. Pack into suitable containers, seal and label. Freeze for up to 6 months.
BEAN, BROAD	Shell beans and after washing blanch in boiling water for 1 1/2 minutes. Cool in iced water for 1–2 minutes. Place on tray in a single layer and freeze for 30 minutes. Pack into freezer bags, remove air, seal and label. Freeze for up to 6 months.
BEAN, FRENCH, CLIMBING, DWARF	Remove any strings and remove ends. Blanch for 2 minutes and cool in iced water for 2 minutes. Drain, spread on tray in a single layer and freeze for 30 minutes. Pack into freezer bags, remove air from bags, seal and label. Freeze for up to 6 months.
BEET	Only freeze young tender beet, not more than 2–3 in across. Cook until tender and slice, chop or leave whole. Cool and transfer to plastic containers, cover with lids and label. Freeze for up to 6 months.
BROCCOLI	Choose tender young heads with no flowers and tender stalks. Wash well and divide into sprigs. Blanch for 3 minutes in boiling water. Cool in iced water for 3 minutes. Drain and spread on tray in a single layer. Cover with plastic wrap to stop the strong smell of broccoli penetrating the freezer, and freeze for 30 minutes. Pack in freezer bags, remove air from bags, seal and label. Freeze for up to 6 months.
BRUSSELS SPROUT	Remove outer leaves and cut a cross at the stem end of sprout. Wash thoroughly and then blanch for 3 minutes. Cool in iced water for 3 minutes, drain and spread on tray in a single layer. Cover with plastic wrap to prevent strong odor of sprouts penetrating the freezer. Freeze for 30 minutes, remove from tray and pack into plastic bags. Remove air from bags, label and seal. Freeze for up to 6 months.
CABBAGE	Remove outer leaves and wash the remainder. Cut into thin wedges or shred. Blanch for 1 1/2 minutes if shredded, or 2 minutes if cut into wedges. Chill in iced water for 1–2 minutes. Drain and pack in freezer bags, label and seal. Freeze for up to 6 months.
CARROT	Wash and scrub carrots and cut large carrots into pieces. Blanch for 3 minutes in boiling water. Chill in iced water for 3 minutes, drain well. Spread on a tray in a single layer and freeze for 30 minutes. Pack in freezer bags, remove air from bags, label and seal. Freeze for up to 6 months.
CAULIFLOWER	Divide into florets and wash. Blanch for 3 minutes in boiling water. Chill in iced water for 3 minutes. Drain and place on a tray in a single layer. Cover with plastic wrap to prevent strong odor of cauliflower penetrating the freezer. Freeze for 30 minutes. Transfer to freezer bags, remove air from bags, label and seal. Freeze for up to 6 months.
CELERY	Use young tender stalks. Remove any string and wash and cut into 1 in pieces. Blanch for 2 minutes in boiling water. Chill in iced water for 2 minutes. Drain and place on tray in a single layer. Freeze for 30 minutes. Pack freezer bags, remove air, label and seal. Freeze for up to 6 months.
CHAYOTE	Cook sliced chayote until tender in boiling water. Drain well, then mash and cool. Pack into plastic containers with well-fitting lids, leaving space at the top. Freeze. Alternatively, roast the whole chayote, with seeds removed, in a moderate oven until just tender. Cool, pack in containers, leaving room at the top, seal and label. Freeze for up to 6 months.
CHILIES	Remove seeds, wash, dry and spread on a tray in a single layer. Freeze 30 minutes, pack in freezer bags, remove air, seal and label. Freeze for up to 6 months.

VEGETABLES

NAME		TO FREEZE
CHINESE BROCCOLI		Remove any coarse leaves and thick stems. Wash and blanch in boiling water for 2 minutes. Chill in iced water for 2 minutes. Drain and spread on a tray in a single layer for 30 minutes. Pack in freezer bags, remove air, seal and label. Freeze for up to 6 months.
CHINESE CABBAGE		Only freeze crisp and young cabbage. Wash and shred finely. Blanch for 1½ minutes. Chill in iced water for 1–2 minutes. Drain, and place in freezer bags, label and seal. Freeze for up to 6 months.
CHINESE SPINACH		Wash and trim leaves off stalks. Blanch for 1 minute. Chill in iced water for 1 minute. Drain, pack in freezer bags and remove air from bags; seal and label. Will freeze for up to 6 months.
CUCUMBER		Peel and chop in food processor. Pack into plastic containers with well-fitting lids, label and freeze. Freeze for up to 3 months.
EGGPLANT		Cut into slices, sprinkle with salt and allow to stand for 20 minutes. Drain off excess liquid and fry eggplant gently in butter or margarine until just tender. Cool, then pack in plastic containers, seal and label. Will freeze for up to 3 months.
ENDIVE		Do not freeze.
FENNEL		Use fresh young stalks. Wash thoroughly. Blanch for 3 minutes. Chill in iced water for 3 minutes. Drain, pack in freezer bags and remove air from bags. Will freeze for up to 6 months.
GARLIC		Place cloves, separated from bulbs, in freezer bags. Remove any excess air from bag, seal and label. Freeze for up to 3 months.
GINGER		Separate ginger into convenient-sized knobs. Place in freezer bags. Remove excess air from bags, seal and label. Freeze for up to 6 months.
JERUSALEM ARTICHOKE		Peel and slice. Place in cold water with the juice of ½ lemon to prevent discoloration. Blanch for 2 minutes in boiling water. Cool in iced water for 2 minutes. Drain and spread on tray in a single layer. Freeze for 30 minutes. Pack into freezer bags, remove air, seal and label. Freeze for up to 6 months.
KOHLRABI		Wash well, peel and cut into pieces. Blanch for 3 minutes. Chill in iced water for 3 minutes. Drain and spread on a tray in a single layer. Freeze for 30 minutes. Pack in freezer bags, remove air, seal and label. Freeze for up to 6 months.
LEEK		Remove tough outer leaves, wash remainder. Cut away green part of stem, slice white flesh, or cut in halves lengthwise. Blanch 2 minutes (slices), or 3 minutes (halves); chill in iced water 2–3 minutes. Freeze on trays in single layer 30 minutes. Remove, pack in freezer bags, expel air, seal and label. Freeze for up to 6 months.
LETTUCE		Do not freeze.
MARROW SQUASH		Peel, cut into pieces and cook in boiling water until just cooked. Cool and place in freezer bags, remove air from bags, seal and label. Alternatively, bake in oven until almost cooked. Cool, package in freezer bags, seal and label. Freeze for up to 3 months.

NAME		TO FREEZE
MUSHROOM		Cultivated mushrooms need no preparation. Pack clean mushrooms in freezer bags. Remove air from bags, seal and label. Freeze for up to 6 months.
OKRA		Wash well and trim off stems. Blanch in boiling water for 3–4 minutes. Cool in iced water for 3–4 minutes, drain and pack in freezer bags. Remove air from bags, seal and label. Freeze for up to 6 months.
ONION		Peel, chop or cut into rings. Wrap in layers of plastic wrap, place in a plastic container. Label and freeze for up to 3 months. Alternatively, package small onions in their skins in freezer bags. Remove air from bags, label and seal. Freeze for up to 3 months.
PARSNIP		Peel and dice. Blanch for 2 minutes, chill in iced water for 2 minutes, then spread on a tray and freeze for 30 minutes. Pack into freezer bags, remove air, label and seal. Freeze for up to 6 months.
PEA		Shell, wash and blanch for 1 minute. Chill in iced water for 1 minute, drain, spread on a tray. Freeze for 30 minutes. Pack into freezer bags, remove air, seal and label. Freeze for up to 6 months.
PEPPER		Wash, remove seeds and cut into slices or leave whole. Place on a tray in a single layer. Freeze for 30 minutes. Pack in freezer bags, remove air, label and seal. Freeze for up to 6 months.
POTATO		There are a number of ways of freezing potatoes. (a) Scrub new potatoes. Cook in boiling water until almost cooked. Drain, cool, pack in freezer bags. Seal, label and freeze for up to 6 months. (b) Prepare chips and deep fry for about 4 minutes until cooked, but not brown. Drain and cool on paper towels. Place on a tray in a single layer and freeze for 30 minutes. Pack in freezer bags, remove air, label and seal. Freeze for up to 3 months. (c) Potatoes may also be mashed and then frozen for up to 3 months.
PUMPKIN		Peel and cook in boiling salted water until tender. Mash, cool, then pack into plastic containers, leaving headspace. Freeze for up to 3 months. Alternatively, peel and cut into pieces. Bake until almost cooked. Pack into freezer bags when cool, remove the air, seal and label. Will freeze for up to 3 months.
RADISH		Do not freeze.
RUTABAGA		Only use tender, young rutabaga. Cut to required size and blanch for 3 minutes. Chill in iced water for 3 minutes. Drain, place pieces on a tray in a single layer and freeze for 30 minutes. Pack in freezer bags, remove air, seal and label. Freeze for up to 6 months.
SHALLOT		Separate cloves from bulb. Place in freezer bags, remove excess air. Freeze for up to 3 months.
SNOW PEA		Wash well and trim leaves from stalks. Blanch in small quantities of boiling water for 1 minute. Chill in iced water for 1 minute, drain, then pack in freezer bags or containers. Remove air from plastic bags, label and date bags or containers and freeze. Will freeze for up to 6 months.
SPINACH		Use tender pods. Wash and trim. Blanch for 30 seconds. Chill in iced water for 30 seconds. Drain, pack in freezer bags, remove air, seal and label. Freeze for up to 6 months.

VEGETABLES

NAME		TO FREEZE
SQUASH		Peel and cook in boiling salted water until tender. Mash, cool and pack into freezer containers leaving room at the top for expansion. Seal and label. Freeze for up to 3 months.
SUGAR SNAP PEA		Remove pods, wash and blanch for 1 minute. Chill, drain and spread on a tray. Freeze for 30 minutes, then pack in plastic bags, remove air from bags, seal and label. Will freeze for up to 6 months.
SWEET CORN		Remove leaves and threads and cut off top of cob. Wash, blanch a few cobs at a time for 5–7 minutes, depending upon size. Chill in iced water for 5–7 minutes, drain, then wrap each cob in plastic wrap. Pack wrapped cobs in freezer bags, remove air from bags, label and seal. Freeze for up to 6 months.
SWEET POTATO		After scrubbing and peeling, bake or roast until just tender. Drain on absorbent paper and cool. Pack into plastic bag or container. If using plastic bags ensure that air is removed before sealing. Label and date. Will freeze for up to 3 months.
SWISS CHARD		Wash well and trim leaves from stalks. Blanch in small quantities of boiling water for 1 minute. Chill in iced water for 1 minute, drain, then pack in freezer bags or containers. Remove air from plastic bags, label and date bags or containers and freeze. Will freeze for up to 6 months.
TARO ROOT		Peel and cut into pieces. Blanch for 3 minutes in boiling water, chill in iced water for 3 minutes. Spread on a tray in a single layer and freeze for 30 minutes. Remove from freezer and pack in freezer bags. Remove air from bags, label and seal. Freeze for up to 6 months.
TOMATO		There are various ways of freezing tomatoes. (a) Wash, remove stems, cut into halves or quarters or leave whole. Dry and pack into freezer bags. Remove air, label and seal. Freeze for up to 6 months. (b) Dip into boiling water for 1 minute, remove and peel. Place whole tomatoes on a tray and freeze for 30 minutes. Place in plastic bags, remove air, seal and label. Freeze for up to 6 months. (c) Simmer chopped tomatoes in a pan for 5 minutes or until soft. Push through a sieve or food mill to remove skins and seeds. Cool, then pack in plastic containers, leaving space at the top of container. Will freeze for 6 months.
TURNIP		Peel and trim young, tender turnips. Cut to required size and blanch for 3 minutes, chill in iced water for 3 minutes. Drain, place pieces on a tray in a single layer and freeze for 30 minutes. Pack into plastic bags, remove air, seal and label. Freeze for up to 6 months.
WATER CHESTNUT		Bring chestnuts to the boil. Drain and peel off shells. Pack in freezer bags or plastic containers, remove air, seal and label. Freeze for up to 6 months.
WHITE RADISH		Do not freeze.
WITLOOF		Wash well. Blanch for 3 minutes. Drain, place on a tray in a single layer and freeze for 30 minutes. Pack into plastic bags, remove air, seal and label, or pack in containers leaving some space at top. Freeze for 2–3 months.
ZUCCHINI		Slice into 1 in slices without peeling, then sauté gently in a little melted butter until barely tender. Cool, then pack into plastic containers, leaving space at the top of the container. Freeze for up to 3 months.

HARVESTING CHART

PLANT COMMON NAME	SUITABLE CLIMATE	SPRING			SUMMER			AUTUMN			WINTER		
		EARLY	MID	LATE	EARLY	MID	LATE	EARLY	MID	LATE	EARLY	MID	LATE
Artichoke	●●●	●●	●●	●●	●●			●	●	●	●		
Asparagus	●●	●●											
Bean	○○●●	○●	○●	○○●	○○●	○○●	○○●	○○	○	○	○	○	○
Beet	●●●●	●●●	●●●	●●●	●●●		●●	●●●	●	●●	●	●	●
Broad bean	○○●●	○●	○	○	●	●	●						○○○
Broccoli	●●●	●	●	●	●	●	●	●	●	●●	●	●	●
Brussels sprout	●●●					●	●●	●●●	●●	●●	●●	●	●
Cabbage	●●●●	●●	●●	●●	●●	●●	●●	●●●	●●●	●●●	●●	●	●
Carrot	●●●●	●●	●	●●	●●	●●●	●●●	●●●	●●●	●●●	●●●●		●●
Cauliflower	○○●●						●●	●●●	●●	●●●	●●●		
Celery	○○●●				●	●	●●●	●●●●	●●	●●	●●	○	○
Chayote	○●	○	○	○	○●	●	●						
Chilies	○●●	○	○	○○●	●●●	○●	○●	○	○	○	○	○	○
Chinese broccoli	○●●				○	○	○○●	●●●	●●●	●●●	○		
Chinese cabbage	○○●●	○○●	○○●	○○●	○○●	○○●●	○○●●	○○●	○	○	○	○	○
Chinese spinach	○●			○	○●	○●	○●	○●					
Cucumber	○○●●	○	○	○●	○○●	○○●	○○●	○	○	○	○	○	○
Eggplant	○●●	○	○	○	○●	○●	○○●	○●●	○	○	○	○	○
Endive (curly)	○○●●	○○●	○○●	○○●	○○●	○○●●	○○●●	○●			●	●	●
Fennel	○●●				○○●	○○●	○○●						
Garlic	○●●●			○●	○○●	○○●	○○●●						
Ginger	○●			○	○	○	○●						
Jerusalem artichoke	○●●	○	○	○○●	○●								
Kohlrabi	○○●●	●	●	○●	●	○●	○○●	○○●	○○●	○○●			
Leek	○○●●			○	○●	○●	○○●	○○●●	○○●	○○●	○●		
Lettuce	○○●●	○○●	○○●	○○●	○○●●	○○●●	○○●●	○○●●	○○●	○○●	○○●	○○●	○○●

CLIMATE KEY	○ TROPICAL	● SUBTROPICAL	◐ WARM	◑ COOL	● COLD

PLANT COMMON NAME	SUITABLE CLIMATE	SPRING			SUMMER			AUTUMN			WINTER		
		EARLY	MID	LATE	EARLY	MID	LATE	EARLY	MID	LATE	EARLY	MID	LATE
Marrow squash	●●●●	●	●	●●	●●	●	●●●	●	●	●	●	●	●
Mushroom	○○○●	○○○●	○○○●	○○○●	○○○●	○○○●	○○○●	○○○●	○○○●	○○○●	○○○●	○○○●	○○○●
Okra	○○●	○	○	○	○○	○○	○○○	○○●	○	○	○	○	○
Onion	○○●●	○○●	○●	○●	○●	●	●						○●
Parsnip	○○●●	○	○	○●	○○●	○●	○●●	○○●			○	○	○●●
Pea	○○●●	○●	●	●	●		●●	○			○	○	○
Pepper	○○●	○	○	○○●	○○●	○○●	○○●	○	○	○	○	○	○
Potato	○○●●	○	○	○●	○○●	○●	○●	●●		○●	○	○	○
Pumpkin	●●●●	●	●	●	●●	●●	●●●	●●●●	●●	●			●
Radish	○○●●	○●	○●	○●●	○○●	○○●	○○●	○○●	○○●	○○●	○●	○	○
Rutabaga	●●●●	●							●	●●●	●●		
Shallot	○○●●	○○●	○○●	○○●	○○●	○○○●	○○○●						
Snow pea	●●●●	●●●	●●	○●	●●	●●	●●	●●●	●●●	●●●	●	●	●
Spinach	●●●●	●			●●	●●	●●	●●●	●●	●●●	●●●	●●	●●
Squash	●●●●	●	●	●●	●●●	○●●●	○●●●	●●	●	●	●	●	●
Sugar snap pea	●●●●	●●●	●●	○●	●	●	●●	●●●	●●●	●●●	●	●	●
Sweet corn	○○●	○	○	○	○○●	○○●	○○●	○	○	○	○	○	○
Sweet potato	○●			○	○	○	○●	○●	◐	○	○		
Swiss chard	●●●●	●●●	●●●	●●●	●●●	●●●	●●●	●●●	●●	●●	●	●	●●
Taro root	○●	○	○	○●	○●	○●	○●	○	○	○	○	○	○
Tomato	○○●	○●	○●	○●	○○●	○○●	○○●	○	○	○	○	○	○
Turnip	●●●●	●	●	●	●	●	●	●●	●●	●●●	●		
Water chestnut	○●						○●	○●	○	○			
White radish	○○●●	●	●	●		●	○	○●	○●	○●	○	○	○
Witloof	○○●●	○						○	○	○●	○○○●	○○○●	○○●
Zucchini	●●●●	●	●	●●	●●●	○●●●	○●●●	●	●	●	●	●	●

HARVEST RECIPES

Everyone who grows their own vegetables knows that after the excitement of the first few meals using home-grown produce, boredom can set in. A chorus of "not parsnips again!" from the family is enough to break a gardener's heart. Fortunately there are lots of ways to use a surfeit of vegetables. These recipes allow you to preserve vegetables—some for just a few days, some for several months—which means you can enjoy the produce of your garden long after harvesting.

FRIED ARTICHOKES WITH GARLIC AND CHILI

7 medium artichokes

juice of 2 large lemons

2 tablespoons flour

2–3 tablespoons olive oil

salt, to taste

3–4 whole garlic cloves, peeled

2 tablespoons capers, drained

2–3 chilies, finely chopped

2 cups virgin olive oil

1. Remove all hard outer leaves from artichokes until only a few light green inner leaves and artichoke hearts remain. Using a sharp knife, cut tops from leaves. Brush all cut areas with lemon juice to prevent any discoloration. Dust artichokes in flour; shake off excess.
2. Heat oil in large frying pan; add artichokes and cook until soft. Remove artichokes from pan, drain well on paper towels and sprinkle with salt.
3. Pack artichokes, garlic, capers and chili into large glass jar. Cover with virgin olive oil. Cool completely, then refrigerate.

NOTE: Artichokes will keep 4–5 weeks in the refrigerator.

GREEN BEAN RELISH

2 lbs green beans

3 onions

6¼ cups malt vinegar

1½ cups sugar

1 teaspoon salt

½ teaspoon pepper

1 tablespoon flour

1 tablespoon dry mustard

1 teaspoon turmeric

¼ cup malt vinegar, extra

1. Trim beans and slice diagonally. Peel and thinly slice onions.
2. Combine vinegar, sugar, salt and pepper in large pan. Bring to the boil, stirring, until sugar dissolves. Add the prepared beans and onions; bring to the boil, then reduce heat and simmer, uncovered, until the beans are just tender.
3. Blend flour, mustard and turmeric with extra vinegar. Add to pan and stir over high heat until mixture boils and thickens. Reduce heat and simmer for 5 minutes. Spoon mixture into warm, sterilized jars and seal. Store until required.

BEET ORANGE CHUTNEY

1 lb beets

2 large green apples, peeled and cored

2 oranges

1 cup firmly packed soft brown sugar

1 cup red wine vinegar

1. Preheat oven to moderate 350°F Brush a baking tray with oil. Trim leafy tops from beets and wash thoroughly. Place beets on prepared tray and bake for 1 hour 15 minutes or until very tender. Set aside to cool. Peel skins from beets and cut flesh into small cubes.
2. Cut apples into small cubes. Peel oranges, removing pith from peel and flesh. Cut the peel into thin strips and chop orange flesh, discarding any pips. Place prepared orange rind and flesh in a large pan; add apple, sugar and vinegar. Stir over medium heat until boiling. Reduce heat and simmer, covered, for 30 minutes.

3. Add the cubed beets and simmer for another 15 minutes. Cool slightly and spoon the chutney carefully into warm sterilized jars and seal.

NOTE: Chutney will store for up to 6 months.

PICKLED BEETS AND EGG

12 baby beets

1 bunch dill, chopped

8 hard-boiled eggs, peeled

8 black peppercorns

2 cloves garlic, finely sliced

2 cups red wine vinegar

4 tablespoons sugar

salt, to taste

1. Trim beets, leaving 2 in stalk intact; leave root whole. Wash thoroughly and place in large pan; cover with water and bring to boil. Reduce heat and simmer, covered, 1 hour or until beets are tender. Remove from pan and cool. Reserve 1 cup cooking liquid.
2. Remove skin from beets and break off stalks. (Remove roots if you prefer.) Pack beets, dill, eggs, peppercorns and garlic into a large sterilized jar.
3. Combine reserved beet liquid, vinegar and sugar in a bowl. Stir until sugar has dissolved; add salt, to taste. Pour mixture over beet mixture so that it is completely covered. Seal and refrigerate.

NOTE: Store in refrigerator for up to a week. Serve pickled beets with cold sliced ham and a green salad.

PICKLED RED CABBAGE

1 medium red cabbage

3 tablespoons salt

2 tablespoons sugar

pickling spices such as peppercorns,
    juniper berries or allspice berries

1 1/4 cups cider vinegar

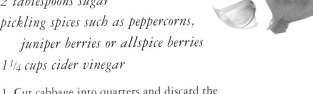

1. Cut cabbage into quarters and discard the tough central core. Shred cabbage finely. Place in a large non-metal dish; add salt and mix through the cabbage. Place a weighted plate on cabbage and leave for 24 hours to draw excess moisture.
2. Rinse cabbage thoroughly and drain on paper towels. Pack tightly into a large, warm, sterilized jar, layering with sugar and spices. Cover with vinegar and seal. Leave for 2–3 weeks before serving.

NOTE: Pickled cabbage will keep for up to 6 months but should be refrigerated once opened. This is a "quick" version of the classic German sauerkraut—a fermented cabbage pickle that is traditionally made in wooden barrels which takes approximately 1 month to prepare.

GARLIC PEPPERS

2 green peppers

2 red peppers

4 cloves garlic, peeled and thinly sliced

1/2 cup sugar

4 cups white vinegar

1 tablespoon salt

1. Cut peppers lengthways into quarters. Remove seeds and membrane. Place peppers in a large pan of boiling water for 1 minute. Remove from pan and cool. Place peppers and garlic in large sterilized glass jar.
2. Combine sugar, vinegar and salt in pan; stir over medium heat until sugar and salt have dissolved.
3. Pour hot liquid over peppers; seal and store for at least 1 week before opening.

NOTE: Garlic pepper stores well for up to 6 months. Serve with other antipasti.

RED PEPPER SOUP

2 large red peppers

1 tablespoon oil

1 large onion, chopped

2 cloves garlic, chopped

1 teaspoon grated ginger

2 x 14 oz cans tomatoes, crushed

5 cups chicken stock

sour cream, to serve

1. Cut peppers into pieces, removing seeds and membrane, and flatten out. Place under a hot grill and cook until skins are black (about 5 minutes). Remove from heat and cover with a damp towel. Allow to cool, then peel off skins and discard.
2. Heat oil in a pan. Add chopped onion, garlic and ginger; cook over medium heat for 5 minutes. Add peppers, tomato and stock, bring to the boil and simmer for 20 minutes. Allow to cool.
3. Process soup in blender until smooth. Reheat before serving with a swirl of sour cream, if desired.

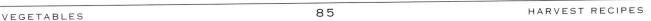

CARROT AND RHUBARB PRESERVE

2 lbs carrots, peeled and thinly sliced

2 lbs rhubarb, thinly sliced

2 lbs sugar

1. Cook carrots in a large pan of boiling water 10 minutes or until tender. Drain, reserving 1 cup cooking liquid.
2. Process carrots and reserved liquid in food processor until smooth. Transfer to large pan; add rhubarb and sugar.
3. Stir mixture over medium heat until sugar has dissolved. Bring to the boil, reduce heat and simmer, uncovered, 20 minutes or until thickened. Spoon cooled mixture into warm, sterilized jars and seal.

NOTE: Will store for up to 1 month in the refrigerator. Use preserve as a filling for sponge cakes or fruit tarts.

PICKLED CAULIFLOWER

1/2 cup salt

5 cups water

1 large cauliflower

5 cups cider vinegar

2 tablespoons sugar

1 teaspoon whole cloves

1 teaspoon whole allspice

1 teaspoon peppercorns

2 cinnamon sticks

5 dried red chilies

6 radishes

1. Combine salt and water in large pan and stir over low heat until salt is dissolved. Chop cauliflower coarsely. Place cauliflower in large bowl and cover with salted water. Cover with dry cloth and stand overnight. Drain.
2. Place vinegar, sugar, cloves, allspice, peppercorns, cinnamon and chilies into a pan. Bring slowly to boil and simmer, covered, for 15 minutes. Strain and retain liquid and spices separately.

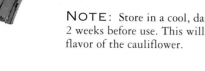

3. Chop radishes and combine with drained cauliflower. Pack into warm, sterilized jars and add reserved whole cloves, allspice, peppercorns, cinnamon and chilies. Return pickling mixture to heat and bring to the boil. Pour boiling liquid over vegetables and seal. When cool, label and date.

NOTE: Store in a cool, dark place for 2 weeks before use. This will enhance the flavor of the cauliflower.

GREEN CURRY PASTE

2 tablespoons oil

2 large onions, finely chopped

2 tablespoons ground coriander

20 large green chilies

2 tablespoons grated fresh ginger

8 cloves garlic, peeled

2 in piece lemon grass

1/2 teaspoon fish sauce

1/3 cup lemon juice

1/2 teaspoon superfine sugar

salt, to taste

1/4 cup oil, extra

1. Heat oil in large frying pan; add onion and cook 3 minutes or until softened. Add coriander and cook 1 minute.
2. Cut chilies in half lengthwise and remove seeds and membrane. Chop finely and place in food processor; add onion mixture, ginger, garlic, lemon grass and fish sauce. Process 30 seconds or until almost smooth.
3. Add juice, sugar and salt and process briefly. With motor constantly running, add oil in a slow stream until well combined. Spoon into warm, sterilized jar and seal.

NOTE: Paste will keep in refrigerator for up to 10 days.

CHILI OIL

2 1/2 cups vegetable oil

3 fresh whole chilies

1 cinnamon stick

2 teaspoons black peppercorns

fresh, whole pieces of flavorings—herbs or whole spices, as desired

1. Heat the oil in a large heavy-based pan. Add the chilies, cinnamon stick and peppercorns. Remove from heat then cover and leave to stand for 2–3 days.
2. Strain the oil into a sterilized bottle. Add fresh, whole flavorings to bottle.
3. Seal and label. Store in a cool, dark place.

NOTE: Fresh herbs such as rosemary, basil, sage or lemon grass may be substituted for the chilies.

CHAYOTE CHUTNEY

5 medium chayotes

2 onions

8 oz dates

1 cup dried apricots

7 oz dried apples

1 cup raisins

1 cup golden raisins

1 cup soft brown sugar

1/2 teaspoon cayenne pepper

3 cups malt vinegar

1. Wash, peel and remove seed from chayotes. Finely chop chayotes, onions, dates, apricots and apples; place in a large pan with both types of raisins.
2. Add sugar, pepper and vinegar. Stir over medium heat until sugar has dissolved. Bring mixture to boil, reduce heat and simmer, uncovered, 60 minutes or until thick. Stir occasionally.
3. Remove from heat; stand mixture 5 minutes before spooning into warm, sterilized jars; seal.

NOTE: Chutney will store for 2–3 months but should be refrigerated once opened.

MUSTARD PICKLE

3 medium Lebanese cucumbers, chopped

1 large onion, chopped

7 oz cauliflower, cut into tiny florets

1 large green pepper, chopped

2 tablespoons salt

2 teaspoons brown mustard seeds

2 tablespoons mustard powder

1/2 teaspoon turmeric powder

1 bay leaf

1 cup malt vinegar

1/4 cup sugar

1 tablespoon corn starch

2 tablespoons water

1. Combine the cucumber, onion, cauliflower and pepper in a large non-metal bowl. Sprinkle with salt, leave to stand overnight.
2. Wash and drain the vegetables, rinsing thoroughly to remove all salt. Place in a large heavy-based pan. Add the mustard seeds, mustard powder, turmeric, bay leaf, vinegar and sugar. Stir over low heat until mixture boils. Simmer, uncovered, for 8–10 minutes, or until vegetables are tender.

3. Combine corn starch and water in a small mixing bowl. Add to pan and stir through the vegetables quickly. Bring to the boil, then remove from heat once the mixture has thickened.
4. Spoon into hot, sterilized jars and seal immediately. Label and date when cool.

OLD-FASHIONED BREAD AND BUTTER CUCUMBERS

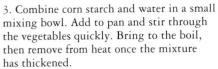

2 lbs green cucumbers, washed and thinly sliced

2 large white onions, cut into thin wedges

2 tablespoons salt

5 cups sugar

1 1/2 cups white wine vinegar

1 tablespoon mustard seeds

1 teaspoon turmeric

1/4 teaspoon cayenne pepper

1. Combine green cucumbers, onion wedges and salt in a bowl. Add enough water to completely cover. Let stand for 2 hours. Drain thoroughly on paper towels.
2. Place sugar, vinegar, mustard seeds, turmeric and cayenne pepper in a large heavy-based pan. Cook, stirring, over medium heat until sugar has dissolved. Add cucumber and onion mixture. Cover, reduce heat and cook gently for 10 minutes, stirring occasionally, until cucumber becomes transparent. Remove from heat.
3. Cool for 15 minutes. Spoon into sterilized jars and seal. Allow to stand for 1 week before using.

EGGPLANT RELISH

2 large eggplants

1/2 cup oil

4 cloves garlic, crushed

2 green peppers, chopped

2 onions, finely chopped

1/2 cup chopped fresh basil

1. Chop eggplant into small cubes. Heat oil in large pan; add eggplant, garlic, pepper and onion. Cook, stirring, 5 minutes or until softened.
2. Remove from heat; add basil and stir through. Cool mixture; spoon into airtight container and refrigerate.

NOTE: Eggplant Relish will store for up to a week in the refrigerator. Serve with curries or add to sandwiches.

EGGPLANT AND WALNUT PASTE

2 large eggplants

3 tablespoons olive oil

1/2 teaspoon finely chopped chili

3 green peppers, seeded, halved and finely chopped

2 garlic cloves, finely chopped

1 cup walnuts

2 teaspoons sherry

2 tablespoons olive oil, extra

1/2 teaspoon salt

virgin olive oil

1. Preheat oven to moderate 350°F. Cut eggplant in half lengthwise, sprinkle eggplant flesh with salt and allow to stand 10–15 minutes. Rinse well and drain on paper towels. Place eggplant, cut-side up, on a baking tray. Bake 20 minutes or until flesh is soft; cool. Scoop out flesh and place in food processor.
2. Heat oil in frying pan; add chili, pepper and garlic and stir over medium heat until vegetables are soft. Transfer to food processor; add walnuts, sherry, extra olive oil and salt.
3. Process mixture 1–2 minutes or until smooth. Spoon the paste into warm, sterilized jars. Top with a thin layer of virgin olive oil and seal.

NOTE: Keeps 3–4 weeks in the refrigerator.

GARLIC VINEGAR

16 cloves garlic

salt, to taste

4 cups white wine vinegar

1. Peel garlic and crush lightly with a little salt. Place in a large, sterilized, glass container; add vinegar.
2. Seal container and shake well. Store in a cool, dark place 2–3 weeks, shaking the container from time to time.
3. Pour vinegar through cheesecloth-lined funnel into sterilized bottles. Can be used at once.

NOTE: Store vinegar for up to 8 months.

ROASTED GARLIC PASTE

10 whole heads garlic

1/2 cup oil

salt and pepper, to taste

oil, extra

1. Preheat oven to moderate 350°F. Using a sharp knife, cut tops off garlic. Pour olive oil over exposed flesh; season with salt and pepper.
2. Wrap 2 or 3 heads at a time in foil and place in baking dish. Roast 1–1 1/2 hours or until flesh is very soft; cool.
3. Squeeze garlic flesh into sterilized jar; drizzle with a little extra oil to just cover.

NOTE: Garlic paste will keep for 2–3 months in the refrigerator. Use paste in sauces and salad dressings, or serve with roast beef on toasted slices of French bread. Garlic has a much milder flavor once cooked, so do not be alarmed by the quantity of garlic in this recipe.

LEMON GINGER BUTTER

2 lemons

8 oz butter

3 tablespoons grated ginger

2 cloves garlic, crushed

1. Remove peel from lemons and grate finely.
2. Beat butter until light and creamy; add ginger, garlic and lemon peel. Beat until smooth.
3. Using plastic wrap, form into a log shape and refrigerate.

NOTE: Lemon ginger butter can be stored 2 weeks in refrigerator or frozen for up to 3 months. Slice off rounds as they are needed, and return to freezer.

PICKLED GINGER

7 oz fresh ginger

sea salt

1 cup rice wine vinegar

3 tablespoons sugar

red food coloring

1. Peel ginger and cut into thin slivers. Place in a mixing bowl and cover with cold water. Leave to stand for 30 minutes. Drain ginger; place in a pan of boiling water. Bring back to boil, drain and cool in mixing bowl; sprinkle with salt.
2. Combine vinegar and sugar in small pan. Stir over low heat until sugar has dissolved. Add a few drops of red coloring and stir.
3. Pour vinegar and sugar mixture over ginger. Cover with plastic wrap and let stand in a cool, dark place for 2–3 weeks before serving.
4. Place the ginger and pickling liquid into a warm sterilized jar. Seal and label.

NOTE: Store pickled ginger in the refrigerator. Serve with Japanese dishes such as sushi or with chicken or seafood.

JERUSALEM ARTICHOKE RELISH

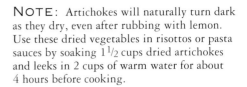

4 lbs Jerusalem artichokes

4 onions

2 green or red peppers

1 teaspoon dill

1 teaspoon mustard seeds

1 teaspoon turmeric

4 cups cider vinegar

1 lb sugar

1. Peel artichokes and chop finely. Chop onions. Remove seeds and membrane from pepper and chop finely. (Vegetables can be processed briefly in food processor, but should retain a coarse texture.)
2. Place in a large pan; add dill, seeds, turmeric, vinegar and sugar. Stir over low heat until sugar has dissolved. Bring to the boil, reduce heat and simmer, uncovered, for 30 minutes or until vegetables are tender.
3. Cool slightly and spoon into warm, sterilized jars; seal.

NOTE: Relish will keep several months but should be refrigerated once opened. Serve with a cheese platter or with roasted meats.

DRIED LEEKS AND ARTICHOKES

juice of 2 medium lemons

8 medium artichokes

1 large lemon

8 leeks

1. Preheat oven to very slow 250°F. Pour about 4 cups water into a bowl and add lemon juice.
2. Using a sharp knife, remove and discard outer leaves of 1 artichoke until only inner leaves and heart are left. Cut lemon in half and rub over artichoke to prevent discoloration. Trim green tops from inner leaves, cut artichoke in half and remove choke using a teaspoon. Rub again with lemon, then put in bowl of water and lemon juice while preparing remaining artichokes in same way.
3. Remove artichokes from water, cut into quarters and rub again with lemon.
4. Discard roots and green leaves from leeks, leaving only white stems. Halve leeks lengthwise, then cut into 1 in slices. Wash thoroughly and drain on paper towel. Arrange leeks and artichokes on wire grill and place on oven rack with artichokes.
5. Leave in oven for about 4 hours, or overnight, until artichokes and leeks are completely dry. Allow to cool, break into pieces using fingers, mix together and store in airtight boxes for up to a year.

NOTE: Artichokes will naturally turn dark as they dry, even after rubbing with lemon. Use these dried vegetables in risottos or pasta sauces by soaking 1 1/2 cups dried artichokes and leeks in 2 cups of warm water for about 4 hours before cooking.

CONFIT OF ROASTED LEEKS

4 lbs young leeks

1/2 cup olive oil

2 teaspoons salt

2 teaspoons sugar

1. Preheat oven to moderate 350°F. Clean leeks thoroughly, discarding roots and leaves. Cut into 1/4 in slices.
2. Layer leeks 3/4 in deep in a well-greased shallow baking tray. Drizzle with olive oil and sprinkle with salt and sugar.
3. Roast, turning often, for 45 minutes to 1 hour, or until leeks appear caramelized and creamy gold.
4. Allow to cool then spoon into dry, sterilized jars; seal.

NOTE: Store roasted leeks in refrigerator for up to 2 weeks. Serve warm or cold in sandwiches, as a pizza topping or to enrich soups or stews.

PICKLED MUSHROOMS

1 1/2 lb mushrooms

1 tablespoon grated fresh ginger

rind of 1 lemon

1 onion, thinly sliced

4 cups white wine vinegar

salt and pepper, to taste

1. Wipe mushrooms with a damp cloth and trim the stalks to level with the cap.
2. Combine mushrooms, ginger, lemon rind, onion, vinegar, salt and pepper in large pan. Bring to the boil, reduce heat and simmer 20 minutes or until tender.
3. Remove mushrooms with a slotted spoon and transfer to warm, sterilized jars. Strain cooking liquid and return to the boil. Pour liquid over mushrooms, covering them well. Seal and refrigerate.

NOTE: Pickled mushrooms will not keep as long as many other types of pickled vegetables. It is best to use them within 2 weeks of bottling.

GUMBO

1 lb okra

14 oz can whole tomatoes, undrained

2 oz butter

1 large onion, finely chopped

1 green pepper, finely chopped

2 short celery stalks, finely sliced

2 cloves garlic, chopped

2 teaspoons tomato paste

2 teaspoons white pepper

2 teaspoons cracked black pepper

1 1/2 teaspoons cayenne pepper

2 teaspoons dried thyme

1/2 teaspoon dried oregano

2 bay leaves

1/4 teaspoon ground allspice

2 teaspoons chili flakes

1 tablespoon Worcestershire sauce

1 cup chicken stock

1. Combine okra and tomatoes in a pan. Bring to the boil, reduce heat and simmer, covered, for 15 minutes.
   2. Melt butter in another large pan; add onion, pepper, celery and garlic and cook slowly 20 minutes or until very tender.
      3. Add okra and tomato mixture to vegetables; add tomato paste, peppers, thyme, oregano, bay leaves, allspice, chili, sauce and stock. Bring to the boil, reduce heat and simmer, uncovered, 15 minutes.

NOTE: This dish can be eaten immediately or frozen in serving portions. Add prawns, chicken, ham, beets or other vegetables. Serve with rice.

PICKLED ONIONS

2 lbs baby onions

1 cup salt

8 cups water

1/2 cup sugar

6 black peppercorns

6 whole cloves

cinnamon stick

4 blades mace (optional)

2 teaspoons whole allspice

2 cups white wine vinegar

red chilies, for bottling

1. Peel onions and place in large bowl; add salt and water and stir well. Cover and allow to stand 2 days, stirring occasionally.
2. Combine sugar, peppercorns, cloves, cinnamon, mace, allspice and vinegar in a large pan. Add onions; stir over low heat until sugar dissolves. Bring to boil, remove from heat and stand 1 hour. Remove onions with a slotted spoon; strain spiced vinegar and reserve liquid.
3. Pack drained onions into warm, sterilized jars, including 2–3 chilies in each jar. Pour vinegar over onions and chilies and seal.

NOTE: Store onions in cool dark place for up to a year. Refrigerate after opening.

PARSNIP CHUTNEY

2 lb parsnips

3 onions

1 orange

1 1/2 cups vinegar

1 cup water

1 1/2 cups soft brown sugar

8 oz dates

1 tablespoon curry powder

1/2 teaspoon garam masala

2 teaspoons salt

1. Peel and finely chop parsnips and onions. Peel orange and shred peel thinly; chop flesh coarsely.
2. Place parsnips, onions, orange rind, vinegar and water in large pan. Bring to boil, reduce heat and simmer, uncovered, 1 hour. Add sugar, dates, curry powder, garam masala and salt; stir over medium heat until sugar dissolves. Bring to boil, reduce heat and simmer, uncovered, until mixture thickens, stirring occasionally.
3. Remove from heat and stand 5 minutes before spooning into warm, sterilized jars; seal.

NOTE: Store for up to six months and refrigerate after opening. Serve with chicken or beef curry.

PUMPKIN JAM

8 oz dried apricots, chopped

4 cups water

1 lb pumpkin, peeled and chopped

1/2 cup orange juice

1 tablespoon chopped glace ginger

1 tablespoon chopped crystallized pawpaw

4 cups sugar

1. Combine apricots and water in bowl; cover and allow to stand overnight.
2. Combine apricots and water, pumpkin, juice, ginger and pawpaw in large pan. Bring to boil, reduce heat and simmer, covered, 20 minutes or until pumpkin is soft. Add sugar, stirring constantly until dissolved. Bring to boil; boil, without stirring, 30 minutes or until jam is thick and falls heavily from a wooden spoon.
3. Spoon into warm, sterilized jars; seal.

NOTE: Store jam up to 2 months in refrigerator. Serve with pumpkin scones.

RADISH TZATZIKI

20 radishes

1 1/2 cups plain yogurt

2 tablespoons lemon juice

salt and pepper, to taste

1. Wash and grate radishes.
2. Combine yogurt and lemon juice in bowl; add radish. Mix well, season to taste. Cover and allow to stand 5 minutes before serving.

NOTE: Serve as a dip or with roast lamb. Can be stored for up to a day in refrigerator.

SWEET CORN RELISH

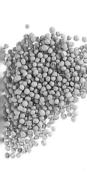

8 ears of corn

2 red peppers

2 green peppers

2 medium onions, finely chopped

8 celery stalks, finely chopped

6 cups cider vinegar

1/2 cup sugar

3 tablespoons mustard seeds

3 teaspoons salt

4 allspice berries

1. Remove and discard husks and silks from corn. Slice kernels from each cob. Remove and discard seeds and membranes from peppers; chop finely.
2. Combine corn kernels, peppers, onion, celery, vinegar, sugar, seeds, salt and berries in large pan. Stir over low heat until sugar has dissolved.
3. Bring mixture to boil, reduce heat and simmer 15–20 minutes or until vegetables are tender, stirring occasionally. Spoon into warm, sterilized jars and seal.

NOTE: Store sweet corn relish for several months in a cool, dry place. Refrigerate after

opening. Serve on cheese sandwiches or combine with mayonnaise and serve with poached eggs.

TOMATO PASTE

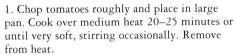

10 lbs ripe tomatoes

1 tablespoon salt

white pepper, to taste

olive oil

1. Chop tomatoes roughly and place in large pan. Cook over medium heat 20–25 minutes or until very soft, stirring occasionally. Remove from heat.
2. Place tomato in food processor and process 30 seconds or until pureed. Return to pan and bring to boil; reduce heat and simmer, uncovered, until reduced by half. Preheat oven to very slow 250°F.
3. Transfer to greased baking dish and bake 4–5 hours or until paste is very thick and concentrated. Add salt and pepper and spoon into warm, sterilized jars. Cover with a thin layer of olive oil and seal.

NOTE: Tomato paste will keep for up to a year in a cool, dry place. Because it is used so often, this is an ideal recipe if you have an over-supply of tomatoes which are on the verge of becoming over-ripe.

TOMATO SAUCE

4 lbs ripe tomatoes, roughly chopped

4 medium brown onions, finely chopped

2 cloves garlic, roughly chopped

1 tablespoon salt

1 tablespoon black pepper

1/2 teaspoon cayenne pepper

6 whole cloves

2 cups soft brown sugar

2 cups white wine vinegar

1. Combine tomato, onion, garlic, salt, peppers and cloves in a large heavy-based pan. Cook gently over medium heat for 45 minutes or until soft.
2. Add sugar and vinegar and continue to cook over low heat until mixture thickens to sauce consistency.
3. Strain mixture through a sieve and pour into warm sterilized jars and seal.

NOTE: Leave for 2 weeks before using. Store in a cool, dry place.

SPICY BARBECUE SAUCE

2 large red peppers, seeds and
    membrane removed, roughly chopped

4 lbs ripe tomatoes, roughly chopped

3 medium onions, finely chopped

3 sticks celery, finely chopped

2 1/2 cups malt vinegar

2 red chilies, finely chopped

3 cloves garlic, crushed

2 teaspoons grated fresh ginger

1 tablespoon fresh coriander leaves,
    shredded

1 teaspoon ground cumin

1 teaspoon mixed spice

2 teaspoons cracked black pepper

1 teaspoon hot English mustard

2 tablespoons paprika

1 teaspoon Tabasco

1 1/2 cups soft brown sugar

1. Combine peppers, tomato, onion, celery,
vinegar, chilies, garlic, ginger, coriander,
cumin, spice, pepper, mustard, paprika and
Tabasco in a large heavy-based pan. Bring to
boil, stirring occasionally over medium heat.
Reduce heat, simmer uncovered for 1 hour.
2. Cool slightly for about 15 minutes, pour
into food processor and puree. Return mixture
to pan. Add sugar and stir over low heat until
sugar is dissolved. Simmer for 30 minutes or
until mixture is thick enough to coat the back
of a spoon.
3. Pour mixture into hot sterilized jars; seal
immediately. Leave 2 days before using.

GREEN TOMATO CHUTNEY

3 lbs green tomatoes, chopped

2 small green apples, peeled and chopped

1 large onion, chopped

1 teaspoon salt

1/2 cup golden raisins

1 teaspoon whole black peppercorns

1 tablespoon brown mustard seeds

2 cups soft brown sugar, lightly packed

2 cups white vinegar

1/2 teaspoon sweet paprika

1. Place all ingredients in a large, heavy-based
pan. Stir over low heat until sugar dissolves.
2. Increase heat to medium and bring mixture

to the boil. Simmer, uncovered, for 1–1 1/2
hours, or until chutney has thickened. Stir
mixture occasionally. Stir more frequently
towards the end of cooking time to ensure
mixture does not stick or burn.
3. Remove from heat, set aside for 5 minutes.
Pour mixture into hot, sterilized jars; seal
immediately. Label and date when cool. Store
in a cool, dark place for up to 12 months.

TOMATO CHILI JAM

2 large red peppers

4 red chilies, finely chopped

4 lbs tomatoes, peeled and chopped

4 green apples, peeled and grated

4 garlic cloves, crushed

1 tablespoon finely grated lemon rind

3/4 cup lemon juice

3 1/2 cups sugar

1. Cut peppers into large pieces and remove
seeds and membrane. Place on a baking tray
and cook under a hot grill 5 minutes or until
skin is completely blackened. Remove from
heat; cover with a clean damp towel and cool
completely. Peel skin from peppers and chop
flesh finely.
2. Place peppers, chili, tomato, apple, garlic
and lemon rind in a large pan. Bring to the
boil, reduce heat and simmer 20 minutes.
3. Add lemon juice and sugar to pan. Stir until
sugar has dissolved. Simmer 1 hour, stirring
occasionally.
4. Remove jam from heat and allow to stand
5 minutes. Spoon jam into warm, sterilized
jars and seal.

NOTE: Store for up to a year.

TO SUN-DRY TOMATOES

Choose firm, ripe Roma tomatoes. Plunge
tomatoes into boiling water, remove
immediately and plunge into cold water; drain
and dry. Cut tomatoes in half lengthwise. Line
racks or deep trays with double layers of
cheesecloth. Arrange tomatoes cut-side up on
racks and place racks outdoors, leaving room
underneath for circulation. (Cover with
netting to protect tomatoes from insects, if
you like.) Tomatoes will take about 3–5 days
to dry out, depending on the weather. Bring
tomatoes in during cool nights or periods of
intense humidity. Turn tomatoes over when
you can see that the moisture on one side has
completely evaporated. Tomatoes are ready
when they have a chewy, slightly leathery
texture. Loosely pack in plastic bags or glass
jars and store for 5–7 days before using,
shaking occasionally. Store firmly packed in
oil in glass containers. Use within a year.

TO OVEN-DRY TOMATOES

Preheat oven to very slow 175°F (lower, if possible). Place prepared tomatoes cut-side up on wire racks in baking trays and place in oven. Leave oven door open slightly and turn on the oven-fan if you have one. Tomatoes will take up to 16 hours to dry. Turn trays frequently and remove pieces as they are done. Apart from their usual uses in sandwiches and on antipasto platters, tomatoes can also be used in slow-cooking dishes such as casseroles.

TURNIP PICKLE

2 small beets

2 lbs turnips, peeled

4 cups white wine vinegar

2–4 tablespoons sugar

2 small chilies

2 bay leaves

2 tablespoons coriander seeds

1. Scrub beets thoroughly, dry and chop finely. Slice turnip thinly.
2. Combine vinegar and sugar in large pan; stir over medium heat until sugar dissolves. Cool.
3. Pack turnip slices, beets, chilies, bay leaves and coriander seeds into warm, sterilized jars; cover with vinegar mixture and seal.

NOTE: Store in a cool, dark place 5 days before use. Store for 3 months in refrigerator.

ZUCCHINI CHUTNEY

3 lbs plums

1 lb zucchini, finely chopped

1 lb onions, finely chopped

1½ cups golden raisins

4 cups soft brown sugar

2 teaspoons ground ginger

1 teaspoon dry mustard

4 cups malt vinegar

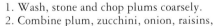

1. Wash, stone and chop plums coarsely.
2. Combine plum, zucchini, onion, raisins, sugar, ginger, mustard and 2 cups vinegar in large pan. Stir over medium heat until sugar dissolves; reduce heat and simmer, uncovered, 30 minutes. Add remaining vinegar and simmer 2 hours, stirring occasionally, until mixture is thick.
3. Spoon into warm, sterilized jars and seal.

NOTE: Store 1 month before using. Store for up to a year in a cool, dry place.

ZUCCHINI PICKLE

3 lbs zucchini

14 oz onions

1 cup salt

10 cups water

4 cups white wine vinegar

7 oz sugar

2 teaspoons mustard seeds

1 tablespoon celery seeds

1 tablespoon allspice berries

1. Slice zucchini thinly. Peel onion and slice thinly. Combine salt and water in a large bowl; add zucchini and onion and leave to stand 3 hours, stirring occasionally. Rinse in cold water, drain well and dry on paper towels.
2. Combine vinegar, sugar, seeds and berries in pan; stir over medium heat until sugar dissolves. Remove from heat, add zucchini and onion and leave to stand 1 hour.
3. Return pan to heat; bring to boil. Boil 3 minutes and remove from heat. Spoon mixture into warm, sterilized jars and seal.

NOTE: Store for 2 weeks before serving. Will keep for up to a year in a cool, dry place.

VEGETABLE STOCK

2 carrots

2 stalks celery, tops left on

1 whole leek

2 tomatoes

1 onion

10 sprigs flat-leaf parsley

1 tablespoon butter

1 tablespoon olive oil

1 bay leaf

2–3 black peppercorns

1 tablespoon grated lemon rind

5 cups water

1. Coarsely chop vegetables and parsley.
2. Melt butter and oil in large pan; add vegetables and stir over medium heat 3–5 minutes or until soft. Add bay leaf, peppercorns, lemon rind and water.
3. Bring stock to boil, reduce heat and simmer, covered, 1 hour. Cool and strain.

NOTE: Stock can be refrigerated for up to 3 days or frozen up to 6 months. A good idea is to freeze stock in ice-cube trays—stock can then be used in small portions as needed. Use any combination of vegetables for this basic stock.

INDEX

A

Agaricus, 46
Allium ampeloprasum Porrum group, 39
Allium ascalonicum, 60
A. cepa, 48, 60
A. giganteum, 35
A. sativum, 35
Alocasia macrorrhiza, 66
Amaranthus tricolor, 29
Apium graveolens, 23
artichoke, 12, 82
  globe, 6, 8, 12, 74, 78
    dried, with leeks, 89
    fried, with garlic and chilli, 84
  Jerusalem, 8, 37, 75, 79, 82
    relish, 89
asparagus, 6, 8, 13, 74, 78, 82
Asparagus officinalis, 13

B

bean, 8, 9, 10, 14–15, 82
  broad, 6, 8, 16, 74, 78, 82
  climbing, 8, 14, *15*, 74, 78
  dwarf, 14, 15, 74, 78
  French, *14*, 74, 78
  green, 8
  relish, green bean, 84
  varieties, 15
beets, 6, 8, 11, 17, 74, 78, 82
  orange chutney, 84
  pickled beets and egg, 85
Beta vulgaris, 17
B. vulgaris var. *cicla*, 65
Brassica napus, var. *napobrassica*, 59
B. oleracea var. *alboglabra*, 27
B. oleracea var. *botrytis*, 22
B. oleracea var. *capitata*, 20
B. oleracea var. *gemmifera*, 19
B. oleracea Gongylodes group, 38
B. oleracea var. *italica*, 18
B. rapa var. *pekinensis*, 28
B. rapa, 69
broccoli, 6, 8, 11, 18, 74, 78, 82
  Chinese, 27, 75, 79, 82
Brussels sprout, 6, 8, 19, 74, 78, 82

C

cabbage, 6, 7, 8, 20, 74, 78, 82
  pickled red cabbage, 85
  Chinese, 8, 28, 75, 79
callaloo *see* taro root
Capsicum annuum, 25

carrot, 6, 8, 11, 21, 74, 78, 82
  baby, 11, 21
  and rhubarb preserve, 86
cauliflower, 6, 8, 22, 74, 78, 82
  pickled, 86
celery, 6, 8, 23, 74, 78, 82
celery cabbage *see* cabbage, Chinese
chard, Swiss *see* Swiss chard
chayote, 8, 24, 75, 79, 82
  chayote chutney, 87
chestnut, water *see* water chestnut
chicory, Brussels, 72
  see also witloof
chilies, 25–6, 74, 79, 82
  chili oil, 86
  green curry paste, 86
  varieties, 23
chives, 9
Cichorium endivia, 33
C. intybus, 72
climate, 7
Colocasia esculenta, 66
container
  gardens, 10
  what to grow in, 11
corn, sweet *see* sweet corn
cress, 10
  mustard, 11
crop planning, 7
cucumber, 6, 8, 30–1, 75, 79, 82
  mustard pickle, 87
  old-fashioned bread and butter, 87
  varieties, 31
Cucumis sativus, 30
Cucurbita, 43, 55, 62, 73
C. maxima, 55
C. moschata, 62
C. pepo, 55, 73
cultivation, 11
Cynara scolymus, 12

D

dasheen *see* taro root
Daucus carota, 21
daikon, Japanese *see* white radish

E

eggplant, 6, 8, 10, 11, 32, 75, 79, 82
  eggplant relish, 87
  eggplant and walnut paste, 88
Eleocharis dulcis, 70

endive, 6, 8, 33, 75, 79, 82
  Batavian, 33
  Belgian, 33, 72
    see also witloof
  curly, 33
escarole *see* endive, Batavian
eschalot *see* scallion

F

fennel, 34, 75, 79, 82
  bronze, 34
  Florence, 34
  sweet, 34
  wild, 34
fertilizers, 7
finocchio *see* fennel, Florence
Foeniculum vulgare, 34
F. vulgare dulce, 34
F. vulgare 'Purpurem', 34
F. vulgare subspecies *vulgaris*, 34
F. vulgare var. *azoricum*, 34

G

gai lun *see* broccoli, Chinese
garden beds, preparation of, 7
garlic, 9, 35, 75, 79, 82
  elephant, 35
  Russian, 35
  roasted garlic paste, 88
  garlic peppers, 85
  garlic vinegar, 88
ginger, 36, 75, 79, 82
  lemon ginger butter, 88
  pickled ginger, 88
gumbo *see* okra

H

Helianthus tuberosus, 37
Hibiscus esculentus syn. *Abelmoschus esculentus*, 47

I

Ipomoea batatas, 64

J

Japanese daikon *see* white radish
Jerusalem artichoke, 8, 37, 75, 79, 82
  relish, 89

K

kailan *see* broccoli, Chinese
kohlrabi, 8, 38, 75, 79, 82

L

Lactuca sativa, 42
lady's finger *see* okra
leek, 6, 8, 39, 75, 79, 82
   dried with artichokes, 89
   confit of roasted leeks, 89
lettuce, 6, 7, 8, 11, 42, 75, 80, 83
   butterhead (cabbage), 42
   cos (romaine), 42
   iceberg, 42
   mignonette, 42
   oak leaf, 11, 42
   varieties, 40–1
Lycopersicon esculentum, 67

M

marrow squash, 43, 75, 79, 83
   vegetable, 6
mushroom, 46, 76, 80, 83
   golden enoki, 46
   pickled, 89
   pine, 46
   shiitake, 46
   varieties, 44–45
   white oyster shimeji, 46

O

okra, 8, 47, 76, 80, 83
   gumbo, 90
onion, 6, 11, 48–9, 76, 80, 83
   pickled, 90
   varieties, 49
   see also scallion; spring onion

P

parsnip, 6, 8, 11, 50, 76, 80, 83
   chutney, 90
Pastinaca sativa, 50
pea, 8, 9, 51–2, 76, 80, 83
   climbing, *52*
   dwarf, 51
   garden, 51
   green, 6
   snow, 6, 51, 76, 80, 83
   sugar snap, 6, 51, 77, 81, 83
   varieties, 52
peppers, 6, 8, 11, 25–6, 74, 78, 82
   chocolate, *5*
   garlic peppers, 85
   red pepper soup, 85
   varieties, 23
permaculture, 10
Phaseolus vulgaris, 14

Pisum sativum, 51
planting
   companion, 8
   and harvesting, 8, 82–3
   space, soil and support, 8
   succession, 8
plants, protection of, 8
potato, 6, 8, 53–4, 76, 80, 83
   sweet *see* sweet potato
   varieties, 54
pumpkin, 6, 8, 55, 76, 80, 83
   bush, 43
   jam, 90
   varieties, 56–7

R

radish, 8, 11, 58, 76, 80, 83
   summer, 58
   tzatziki, 91
   white *see* white radish
Raphanus sativus, 58
R. sativus var. *longipinnatus*, 71
R. sativus var. *radicola*, 71
rhubarb, 6, 8
rutabaga 6, 8, 59, 77, 81, 83

S

scallion, 48
Sechium edule, 24
seeds and seedlings, 8
shallot, 8, 60, 76, 80, 83
   golden, 60
soil
   fertilizers for, 7
   mulching, 7
   pH levels, maintaining in, 6
   and potting mixes, 11
   preparation, 6
Solanum melongena, 32
S. tuberosum, 53
Spinacea oleracea, 61
spinach, 6, 8, 61, 76, 81, 83
   Chinese, 29, 75, 79, 82
sprays
   chamomile tea, 10
   garlic, 9
   general all-purpose, 9
   natural, 9–10
   rhubarb, 9, 10
   soap, 10
spring onion, 11, 48, 49
squash, 8, 62, 77, 81, 83
   button, 43
   spaghetti, 55
   summer, 43, 62
   winter, 55, 62
sweet corn, 6, 8, 63, 77, 81, 83
   relish, 91

sweet potato, 8, 64, 77, 81, 83
Swiss chard, 6, 8, 11, 65, 76,
   80, 83

T

taro root, 66, 77, 81, 83
tomato, 6, 8, 10, 67–8, 77, 81,
   83
   cherry, *10*, 11
   green tomato chutney, 92
   to oven-dry, 93
   spicy barbecue sauce, 92
   tomato chili jam, 92
   tomato paste, 91
   tomato sauce, 91
   to sun-dry, 92
   varieties, 68
turnip, 6, 8, 69, 77, 81, 83
   pickle, 93

V

vegetables
   cooking of, 11
   freezing of, 78–81
   growing of, 5
   harvesting of, 82–3
   preparing a plot for, 6
   storing of, 74–7
   vegetable stock, 93
Vicia faba, 16

W

water chestnut, 70, 77, 81, 83
wong bok
   see cabbage, Chinese
white radish, 71, 77, 81, 83
witloof, 8, 72, 77, 81, 83

Z

Zea mays var. *saccharata*, 63
Zingiber officinale, 36
zucchini, *10*, 73, 77, 81, 83
   Lebanese, 43
   zucchini chutney, 93
   zucchini pickle, 93

This 1997 Crescent edition is published by Random House Value Publishing, Inc.,
201 East 50th Street, New York, N.Y. 10022
http://www.randomhouse.com/

Random House
New York • Toronto • London • Sydney • Auckland

Originally published by Murdoch Books®, a division of Murdoch Magazines Pty Ltd,
213 Miller Street, North Sydney NSW 2060 Australia

Managing Editor, Craft and Gardening: Christine Eslick
Designer: Marylouise Brammer
Series and Cover Design: Jackie Richards
Photographs: Lorna Rose (all unless specified otherwise); Denise Greig (pp. 10L and R, 36, 61L, 73);
Stirling Macoboy (pp. 26R, 47); Reg Morrison (pp. 15R, 23, 31, 40–41, 44–5, 49, 52, 54, 56–7, 68); Joe Filshie (p. 59)
Illustrator: Matthew Ottley
CEO & Publisher: Anne Wilson
International Sales Director: Mark Newman

© Text, photography and illustrations Murdoch Books® 1995

Printed and bound in the United States of America

A CIP catalog record for this book is available from the Library of Congress
ISBN 0-517-18407-9
87654321

Front cover: Cauliflower
Back cover: Sweet corn (top left), tomatoes (top center), white radish (top right),
capsicum (bottom left), spring onions (bottom center), squash (bottom right)
Inside back cover: A brilliant collection of chilies
Title page: Young zucchini with flower attached